D1081654

Getting Started In Permaculture

Over 50 DIY Projects
For House & Garden
Using Recycled Materials

Ross & Jenny Mars

Chelsea Green Publishing
White River Junction, Vermont

©2007 Ross & Jenny Mars
First printed 1994, revised 1998, Candlelight Trust
New edition 2007, Permanent Publications, reprinted 2008
First Chelsea Green Publishing printing April 2008

Designed and typeset by Tim Harland
and John Adams

Our Commitment to Green Publishing
Chelsea Green sees publishing as a tool for cultural change and ecological
stewardship. We strive to align our book manufacturing practices with our
editorial mission and to reduce the impact of our business enterprise on the
environment. We print our books and catalogs on chlorine-free recycled
paper, using vegetable-based inks whenever possible. This book may cost
slightly more because we use recycled paper, and we hope you'll agree that
it's worth it. Chelsea Green is a member of the Green Press Initiative (www.
greenpressinitiative.org), a nonprofit coalition of publishers, manufacturers,
and authors working to protect the world's endangered forests and conserve
natural resources. *Getting Started in Permaculture* was printed on 60# Joy
White, a 30-percent postconsumer recycled paper supplied by Thomson-
Shore.

British Library Cataloguing-in-Publication Data

A catalogue record for this book is available from the British Library

ISBN 978 1 85623 035 3

Disclaimer
Everything in this book has been carfully tested by the authors, but neither the authors
or the publisher shall have liability for any damage or loss (including, without limitation,
financial loss, loss of profits, loss of business or any indirect or consequential loss),
however it arises, resulting from the use of, or inability to use, the information in this book.

Contents

The Authors

Jennifer Mars (Dip. Perm. Des.) is well known in Western Australia as a permaculture teacher. She is a primary school teacher who has contributed to the promotion of permaculture and sustainable living in both country and urban areas. Jenny has helped develop many permaculture designed gardens in schools, nurseries and back yards.

Ross Mars (Dip. Perm. Des.) is an experienced permaculture teacher, designer and consultant. He is a qualified high school teacher and has been actively involved in permaculture education in schools by examining ways of teaching permaculture concepts within the existing curriculum and developing strategies for new lessons in environmental education. Ross is the author of the well known text *The Basics of Permaculture Design* and has also produced an educational video *Passive Solar Design of Buildings* on energy efficient housing.

Acknowledgements

A sincere thank you goes to the following people who have made valuable contributions to this work:

Projects: Pat Scott, Miles Durand, Heather Lamont

Proofreading: Julie Woodman, Pat Scott, Marlyn Wade, Margaret Sampey, David Bayliss, Reny Mia Slay, Patrick Harland

Special thanks to:
    Dora Byrne, Permaculture and Environment Centre, Midvale
    Kevin Smith, Chittering Valley Worm Farm
    Bill Mollison, Permaculture Institute, Tyalgum

Artwork: Patricia Dundas
Cartoons: Kate Dundas
Photographs: Ross and Jenny Mars

Foreword
by Bill Mollison

Since its inception more than 30 years ago, permaculture has focused on positive solutions to the many problems facing the Earth. It encourages people to take responsibility for their own needs and those of their families by growing their own food, reducing their dependence on non-renewable resources and recycling wherever possible. In acquiring practical skills such as gardening, we need some knowledge of the basic techniques. This book, *Getting Started in Permaculture*, demonstrates some methods of organic growing, the use of natural pest control and discusses the responsible use of limited resources which can be recycled and re-used.

Ross and Jenny Mars are well known in Western Australia as teachers and designers of permaculture systems. Here they share their experience and knowledge with a series of activities and projects, each linked to a basic principle of permaculture. So, get your hands dirty – go out and grow your own food and create your own abundance.

Good gardening,

Bill Mollison

About This Book

Getting Started in Permaculture is a book of practical activities which show you how to design and build productive gardens. It outlines the step by step procedures for making herb fertilisers, compost, organic sprays for pest control and much more. The book also discusses how to recycle your soft drink bottles, waste paper and tyres in a number of useful projects such as ponds, fruit fly traps, retaining walls and even a solar still. It is based on the development of Candlelight Farm and the photographs opposite illustrate how it has evolved from a bare paddock into a harmonious, productive living system. Each chapter includes a *Permaculture Perspective* section which explains some of the principles of permaculture design and reasons for advocated actions.

Conventions

This book was originally written for use in the Southern hemisphere and as a result all references to solar orientation were the exact opposite of what we in the North would experience. In this edition all references to North and South have been transposed for Northern hemisphere readers. If you are reading this in the Southern hemisphere please read North for South. All measurements in this book are given in metric.

Conversions

To convert Fahrenheit to Celsius: deduct 32, divide this number by 9 and then multiply by 5.

Measurement Conversion

1 inch = 2.54 centimetres (cm) = 25.4 millimetres (mm)
1 foot = 305 millimetres (mm)
1 yard = 0.914 metre (m)
1 cubic yard = 0.765 cubic metre (m^3)
1 pound = 454 grams (g)
1 acre = 0.405 hectare (ha)
1 gallon = 4.55 litres (l)

Top left: Some of the buildings at Candlelight farm partly obscured by the varied planting. This whole area was originally a barren open field.

Top right: Tyre ponds with hard landscaped edging and safety grids.

Centre: These plants are growing in raised beds made from old tractor tyres.

Bottom left: Ross puts the finishing touches to a geodesic shade house.

Bottom right: Inside their large homemade hot house (polytunnel).

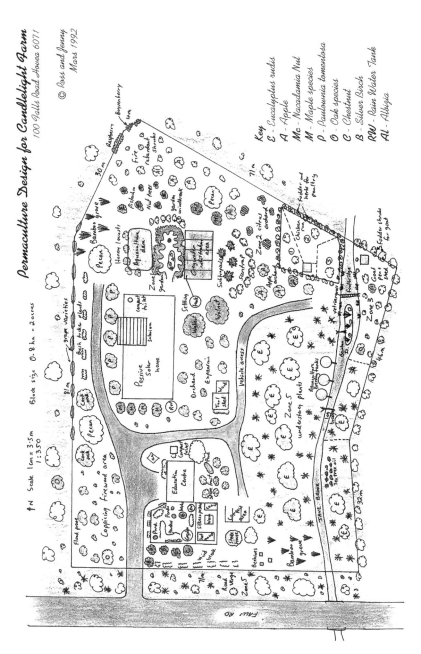

Above: The permaculture design created for Candlelight Farm.

What Is Permaculture?

The term permaculture is a combination of the words permanent and agriculture, or permanent and culture. The difference between permaculture and *normal* agricultural methods is the diversity of organisms in the permaculture system.

Many plants and animals are incorporated in the design; each complementing others, and each having several functions to perform. For example, a pond can be used as an aquaculture centre, a source of water for human consumption or gardens, emergency water for fire control, and for cooling hot winds as part of a climate control method.

Similarly, chickens in a permaculture design might be used for control of pests in the vegetable patch, fruit fly control in an orchard, a source of manure for the garden or methane generator, and for meat or eggs.

Permaculture is an integrated design process where structures, plants and animals are placed in specific areas. It can be applied to both urban and rural properties, from inner city flats to broad acres. Most urban backyards are small and the main activity would be to grow a range of quality, healthy food.

Designs for rural properties are different. Larger-scale permaculture development would include the use of fodder trees for stock, water harvesting methods and water storage, windbreak and shelter areas for animals, agroforestry and alley cropping techniques, land care planting, and commercial food production, such as organic vegetables, nut and fruit trees.

For many people, permaculture is a philosophy and way of life. It is about taking responsibility for your own life and doing the things you feel are important for your own well being, for the well being of others and the well being of our planet.

There are three main ethics which are universally accepted by permaculture practitioners.

These are:

❋ *Earth Care.* This involves taking action to maintain biodiversity, restore damaged and degraded land, conserve natural environments, and use resources ethically.

❋ *People Care.* People's basic needs have to be met in the system. People have to be considered and consulted whenever permaculture systems are designed.

❋ *Surplus Share.* This involves the contribution of surplus time, money and energy to achieve the above two aims of earth and people care. Here, after we have set up our own system and met our own needs and the needs of our family, we can start to help others to achieve their goals.

One of the principles of permaculture is to use the least possible space to produce the greatest amount of food. Food can be grown in and around homes, street verges, parks, schools and vacant land.

Good food leads to good health. Everyone has the ability to produce quality food, in abundance, even in small areas. All you need are the right materials and the right knowledge.

The condition of the soil is crucial to growing good food and everyone knows that working with the soil is good therapy. Compost and earthworms are two ways in which the soil is conditioned to maximise productivity. Earthworms are nature's own ploughs.

Permaculturists usually build no-dig gardens, which means that the ground is not turned over or tilled. Instead, composted materials are placed on the ground and shrubs are planted in this mulch. Earthworms are introduced to aerate the soil, break down the mulch, improve the soil's fertility and enhance micro-organism activity.

Permaculture advocates the use of organic gardening methods; artificial chemical fertilisers, pesticides and herbicides are not recommended. Pest control is achieved by companion planting, organic repellents and other strategies.

Permaculture-designed gardens are based on the natural ecosystems found around the world. We observe the interaction between plants and animals, and of these organisms with their environment, and we strive to design sustainable agricultural systems which are productive, but still in harmony with nature and the land. The design of the system is such that the maximum use of space is made with a complex planting of trees, understorey, shrubs, herbs, underground tuber and root plants and climbers. Plantings are arranged to use every microclimate available, such as the heat that radiates off walls or the humidity and temperature changes near pond edges and hill slopes. You can create your own microclimates for even greater diversity.

External factors such as wind, fire, temperature extremes and light are regulated or utilised by the careful placement of roads, dams, buildings, fences and plants. For example, plants may be used to deflect cold winter winds or hot summer breezes, or to reflect sunlight onto buildings to warm them.

Low maintenance of the system is essential. The amount of human effort and energy expenditure is kept to a minimum. A permaculture design incorporates energy-efficient, intensive systems rather than energy-wasting, extensive systems. Energy, stored in matter recycles on site and less external energy is needed and consumed by the system.

Figure 1. Permaculture is about design. It integrates structures, plants and animals with the needs of humans.

A permaculture system might use a variety of fruit and nut trees which produce year after year, a variety of animals to restore and nurture the land, and a variety of plants which are self-seeding and which can be used as a source of green manure, shade, or to filter and clean water.

What should be stressed is that each permaculture design is unique: there is no one design for all people, properties, soil and land types, or climate. What works in some designs may be inappropriate for others. Plant and animal species are chosen to suit the local conditions as much as possible.

Permaculture designs do take time to establish, but once they are implemented they become more and more productive. As a larger range of usefull products becomes available, the level of maintenance decreases and the system becomes more complex.

Permaculture uses practical techniques to allow you to grow enough food for yourself and family, and even possibly to give away to neighbours. Permaculture employs methods which will help you towards self-sufficiency. However, it does take time. Be patient, and if you need help, you only have to look in *Permaculture Magazine* or contact a Permaculture Association or organisation in your country, for details on what courses are available.

We know that you are keen to get started, so good luck and remember to have lots of fun.

Figure 2. Second hand tyres used to make a planted island in a pond.

Recycling Tyres

Every city has an over-abundance of used tyres. Tyre retailers often pay to have second-hand tyres removed and dumped. Many of these businesses are only too happy to give them away. All you need is to telephone to make arrangements and then get a trailer to pick them up.

Tyres are virtually indestructible; they do not decompose very well and they will last hundreds of years. The number of uses for old tyres is only limited by your imagination.

Here are some easy-to-build projects that involve tyres. They are generally very cheap to put together. Herb mounds, tyre ponds and retaining walls are examples of ways that tyres can be put to use.

A Herb Mound

A herb spiral or mound made from tyres provides bulk, form and shape to the garden bed. Raised mounds permit a variety of microclimates to be produced. For example, one side will have a sunny aspect and hardy Mediterranean herbs such as lavender and rosemary will thrive there. On the opposite side, shade-loving or shade-tolerant herbs such as angelica, mints and comfrey will grow quite well.

What you need

❀ Sand or potting mix and second-hand car or truck tyres.

❀ Selection of herbs. Herbs that can be planted on your mound include: parsley, sage, thyme, marjoram, rosemary, lemon balm, spearmint and other various mints, chives, onion and garlic varieties, comfrey, basil, oregano, garlic, ginger, chamomile, borage, coriander, dandelion, lemon verbena and French sorrel (the more common varieties of sorrel grow to a metre in height).

❀ Manure, such as sheep, horse or chicken.

What you do

❋ Place tyres in the shape of a spiral or pyramid.

❋ Proceed to fill tyres with sand or organic potting mix to eventually cover the tyres and thus form a mound.

❋ Water this well so that the soil completely fills inside each tyre.

❋ Mix chicken manure or sawdust/horse manure with the soil as you fill the tyres.

Water this in thoroughly. You only have to use two shovelfuls of manure for every wheelbarrow load of soil or compost.

❋ It is better to plant herbs a couple of days after the mound is made if you have used relatively fresh chicken manure as it may scald the plants and they could die.

You can plant immediately into an aged manure compost/soil mix.

❋ Herbs that prefer the shade should be planted on the northern side of the herb mound.

For example, various mints (making sure not to plant the mints, such as peppermint and applemint, that spread all over the place), angelica and lemon balm all prefer shade.

Some plants such as rosemary and sage should be planted on the southerly aspect as they are able to tolerate the hot sun.

❋ Water your plants over the next few days so that they become established. A trickle irrigation or drip system is an optional extra that you may want to consider.

Figure 3.
Position the tyres into a mound.

6

A Tyre Pond

Small ponds of water can help produce a variety of foods, e.g. watercress and water chestnuts, and plants such as Azolla can be used as nitrogen fixing mulches. Many more need little or no care after planting in the pond.

What you need

❋ Second hand truck or tractor tyre, with one rim cut away (see page 8 on how to cut a tyre).

❋ Plastic sheet (builder's black).

❋ Flat stone or paving bricks.

❋ Cement (optional).

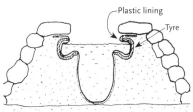

What you do

Figure 4. Tyre pond above ground.

❋ There are two main ways to build the pond. Either the plastic can be laid inside the tyre, permitting the pond to be above ground level (*see figure 4*), or positioned around the outside (*see figure 5*).

This activity assumes that a below ground pond is being built. Alter the following instructions if you are modifying the design.

❋ Dig a hole large enough to fit the tyre in. If you want a deep section, dig the middle deeper.

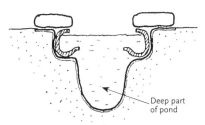

Figure 5. Below ground tyre pond.

❋ Place the plastic over and into the hole.

❋ Carefully lower the tyre onto the plastic. Try not to tear the sheet. Remove any wooden sticks and sharp stones from the hole.

7

* Slowly add water so that the plastic is forced against the base and side walls of the earth.

* At the same time, back fill with clean soil.

* Fold the plastic sheet over the top of the tyre and cut excess away. Level the soil to ground level. Leave the plastic on top of the rim or bend it back (*as shown in figure 6*). Lay the stone or paving bricks around the perimeter in whatever pattern you want. Cementing them together is optional but the finished product will look better and last a lot longer. Cement is made by mixing sand and cement powder in a ratio of 3:1. Add water to make a creamy consistency.

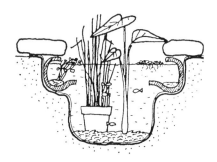

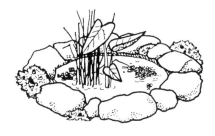

Figure 6.
Finished tyre pond planted up.

Figure 7. Cut the tyre rim near the edge.

Cutting A Tyre

To cut a tyre use a sharp Stanley trimmer and water as the lubricant. A constant drip from a hose on the cutting surface area is sufficient. A jigsaw or sabre saw is quicker and the finished cut is a little neater. Jigsaws can cut through the thin steel belting in some tyres – knives are less successful.

Note: although Stanley is a trademark name it is not so indicated at other times in this book.

Retaining Wall

Retaining walls made from tyres are strong and durable. There is no need to bolt the tyres together as once they are filled with soil you won't be able to move them. However, you could use your drill to make a hole in either side of the tyre wall and bolt one tyre to another for extra stability.

Figure 8. Simple tyre retaining wall.

What you need

✤ Second hand vehicle tyres.

✤ Fill material: rubble, sand or clay.

✤ Optional: concrete, bolts 50mm long and 6mm diameter, electric drill and drill bits (for your bolt size).

What you do

The arrangement of tyres depends on the height of the wall you wish to make. For small walls, say up to one metre, tyres can be stacked on top of one another. Higher walls require that tyres are laid overlapping but offset to each other so that a slope is obtained. This is shown in the diagrams below.

Figure 9. Overlapping tyres allows higher walls to be built.

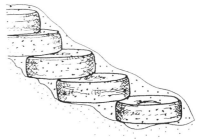

Figure 10. Tyres arranged in a sloping retaining wall.

Other Projects

Here are some other uses for tyres.

Figure 11. Tyre plant protector.

PLANT PROTECTOR
If you use tyres to protect your young plants there are two things to consider. Firstly, water will be retained by the rim, which will increase the humidity and growth of the plants. Use a hole saw or sharp knife to cut a 25mm hole in each tyre on the bottom to allow drainage of excess water.

Secondly, if you want your plants protected from browsing animals you will have to place a wire netting cylinder around the plant and add the tyre for support. Tyres will protect your plants from wind damage and absorb some sun light in winter to keep your plants warm. Don't forget to remove the tyre once the plant is established.

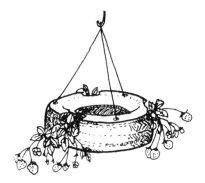

Figure 12. Growing in a hanging tyre.

HANGING BASKET
Drill three holes equally distant from each other in the top of the tyre and thread heavy tie wire through them.

Figure 13. Tyre used as feed trough.

WATER OR FEED TROUGH
A trough or dish like this can be used for water, an animal feed trough or a bird bath. You can cut a piece of wood to fit inside the tyre to act as a base to place the food on or you can put the water or feed in the rim.

TYRE MOAT

Tyre moats are useful to protect young seedlings from snail and slug attack.

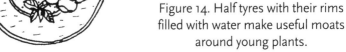

Figure 14. Half tyres with their rims filled with water make useful moats around young plants.

RAISED GARDEN BED

Place several tyres on top of each other. Fill the bottom one or two with rubble or soil. The top two should contain compost to grow your vegetables or strawberries in.

Beware: don't use tyres to grow potatoes and other below-ground or root crops. Leaching of heavy metals and/or toxins may occur, and thus be absorbed in or on plant surfaces.

Figure 15. Four tyre raised bed.

Figure 16.
A tractor tyre compost bin.

COMPOST BIN

A column of large tractor tyres makes an ideal compost bin. Once the compost has been made, dismantle the tyres and move them to another area. Start again.

Caution: tractor tyres are very heavy and need at least two people to move safely.

11

From A Permaculture Perspective

Anything that is placed in a permaculture design is called an element. This term is not to be confused with the chemical elements such as sodium and nitrogen that you may have learnt about at school. The position of any element is crucial in a permaculture design. Elements are positioned depending on the number of times you have to visit them. For example, if you visit your tyre pond every day to pick a couple of leaves of gotu kola (for arthritis treatment and prevention), then it should be located close to the house – in a region we call Zone 1. Zones are discussed on page 66.

Every element in your design should serve at least three functions and every element needs three others to support it. For example, your herb mound might produce edible herbs and vegetables and a selection of medicinal herbs.

It also provides vertical growing space, different aspects for different plants (some herbs prefer shade, others full sun) and differences in soil drainage for particular plants. Besides having many functions, the herb mound also has particular needs which have to be met by other elements placed within the design. For example, other elements in your garden which support your mound could include a tyre pond at the base of the mound to attract predators for pest control, flowers to attract bees, butterflies and moths for the pollination of your herbs and a compost bin to regularly provide material to build and maintain your mound.

Figure 17. Multifunction – recycled tyres used for growing food arranged to create a suntrap.

Recycling Plastic Bottles

There is a dilemma in recycling plastic. On one hand all plastic is recyclable and recycling makes environmental sense. On the other hand, very few industries have the facilities and economic viability to do so.

Some of the activities in these exercises, such as the solar still, are teaching demonstrations – whether for parents to show their children the possibilities of recycling, or teachers to involve students in practical activities. Most activities, however, such as fruit fly traps, mini-greenhouses and slug and snail traps, are appropriate for all gardeners.

Re-using Oil Containers

DUSTPAN & GRAIN SCOOP

What you need

Two simple projects to make are a dustpan and a grain scoop. The scoop can also be made from 2l plastic cordial containers.

- 4l motor oil container.
- Stanley or serrated knife.
- Felt pen or crayon pencil.

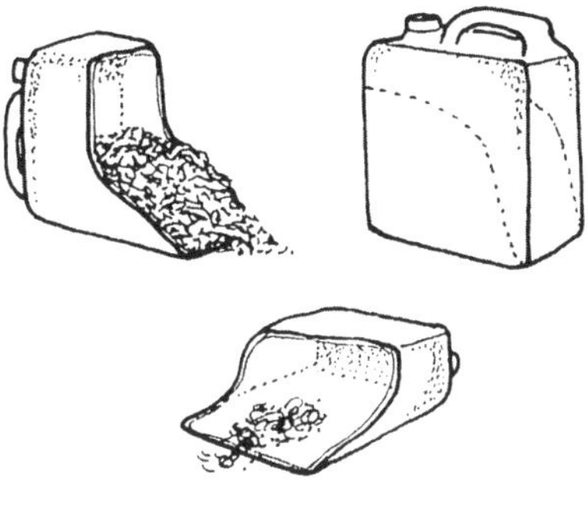

Figure 18. Oil container dustpan and grain scoop.

What you do

- Use a pen to mark a section to be cut away from the container. Figure 18 shows the two different cuts for the dustpan and the scoop – horizontally for the dustpan and vertically for the scoop.
- Use the scissors or serrated knife to cut along the line to make the desired product.

Soft Drink Bottles

What you need (common for all projects)

❀ At least one 2l and one 1.5l plastic soft drink bottle.

❀ Scissors, Stanley or serrated knife.

❀ Felt pen or crayon pencil.

FUNNEL
A basic project to make is a funnel for the transfer of fuel or oil.

What you do

❀ Use the felt pen to mark a straight line about 5cm from the bottom of a bottle.

❀ Use the scissors or knife to cut off the lower part of the bottle.

Figure 19. A soft drink bottle funnel.

❀ The bottom can be used to seal the funnel when not in use. It can also be used to hold nails, nuts, bolts and objects when working on other projects.

FRUIT FLY TRAP
Fruit fly is a serious pest that needs to be controlled in the orchard. Here is a simple project to trap and kill fruit fly. You can find recipes for the baits in the section on organic pest control (see page 25).

Additional materials for this project

❀ Yellow masking tape or electrical insulation tape.

❀ Tie wire or string.

❀ 6mm drill bit.

14

What you do

❋ Cut the bottom from either a 2l or 1.5l soft drink bottle.

❋ Invert the base and push it upwards inside the other part of the bottle. Make sure that it fits tightly.

❋ Drill or burn a small hole, about 6mm diameter, in the inverted base.

❋ Carefully add the bait to the bottle and replace the screw top cap.

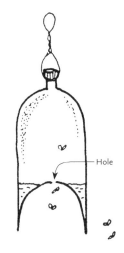

Figure 20. Fruit fly trap.

❋ Wrap yellow masking tape around the join to seal the bottle and to attract the flies.

❋ Use tie wire to support the neck of the bottle and secure it to a fruit tree about one and a half to two metres above the ground.

❋ To clean the trap, unscrew the cap and drain the liquid away – into the compost heap. Give it a good rinse with a jet of water from the hose.

Figure 21. Slater or woodlouse trap.

WOODLOUSE / SLATER TRAP
Woodlice love eating young seedlings. They chew the base and the seedling topples over. This trap uses potato as the bait and attracts and holds them until you lift the trap up. Disposal of woodlice is easy – feed them to quail, chickens or frogs. Alternatively, use them to make a self-insect repellent spray (see page 25).

15

What you do

✤ Cut the bottom off a 2l or 1.5l bottle.

✤ You will have to cover it with black plastic sheet or paint it. A spray can from the hardware store is the easiest and quickest method of covering the base. It has to be dark inside.

✤ Make one or two small holes (about 1cm diameter) around the rim.

✤ Place a potato in an area where slaters are a problem. Cover the potato with an inverted base.

✤ The next morning lift off the base, and collect and dispose of the slaters which have congregated there during the night.

SLUG AND SNAIL TRAP

Bill Mollison has often said, "You don't have a snail problem, you have a duck deficiency." Sometimes ducks are difficult to keep in your backyard; they can destroy the garden with their large feet.

It may be better to make a simple, cheap trap that collects and kills slugs and snails.

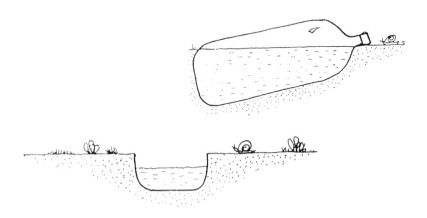

Figure 22. Slug and snail traps baited with stale beer.

What you do

❊ Half fill a soft drink bottle with stale beer. If you can't get hold of some flat beer, use a mixture of one teaspoon of yeast in water.

❊ Bury most of the container on its side in the garden. Leave the cap off so that slugs and snails can enter. Cut some of the neck away if you have large snails that won't fit through the neck.

❊ A different type of trap is made by burying the base of a soft drink bottle to ground level, so that slugs and snails fall into it.

❊ These molluscs are active during the night. Every few days check the trap, pour the yeast mixture and dead snails into the compost heap, refill the bottle and replace the trap.

MINI-GREENHOUSE

Frost-tender seedlings can be protected by enclosing them in a cloche. This is a covering, usually of plastic or glass, which holds the heat around a plant and thus maintains a warm temperature to prevent the untimely death of your beloved plant. Cloches or greenhouses further protect the plant from wind and predators.

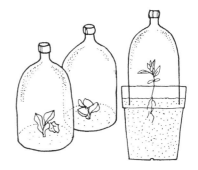

Figure 23. Bottle mini-greenhouses.

What you do

❊ Cut the base off a 2l soft drink container.

❊ For seedlings already in the ground, place the top part of the bottle carefully over the plant. If wind is a problem push some soil around the base to hold the bottle in place.

❊ For flower pots, place the bottle top inside the pot wall and gently push it in. You might damage plant roots if your plant is large and well-established in the pot.

INFILTRATION METER

An infiltration meter is **a** useful tool for determining the ability of your soil to drain water.

This is important if you want to install some type of greywater disposal system. Some local Public Health authorities will want to know the infiltration rate of your soil so that they can calculate the length of the disposal drain system.

What you do

❧ Cut away the base of your 2l cool drink bottle.

❧ Measure 200ml of water in a scientific measuring cylinder or kitchen measuring cup.

❧ Hold or support the bottle, with the screw cap in place, and pour the water into the bottle neck.

❧ Once the water has settled, mark the water level with the felt pen or crayon pencil.

❧ Repeat this until you have level marks up to 1,000ml. Write each volume mark on the side of the bottle.

Figure 24. Testing the infiltration rate in soil and subsoil.

18

❋ Empty the water into a bucket and keep it for the next stage.

❋ Remove the screw cap and place the bottle neck into the soil you wish to test. Support the bottle if you can – a second person helping you is ideal.

❋ Quickly fill the bottle with the litre of water from the bucket and start timing the draining of the water into the soil.

❋ You will find that sandy soils will drain very fast and heavy, clay soils seem to take forever. You don't have to wait for all of the water to drain away. If you know the level you started and finished with, you can calculate the volume you would expect to drain away in an hour. For example, if you started at 1,000ml and after fifteen minutes the level dropped only 200ml then the volume would be 200 x 4 = 800ml per hour (there are 4 x 15 minutes in an hour).

❋ For subsoil drainage, remove the top 15cm of soil and repeat the test.

SEEDLING PROTECTOR

Young plants can be protected from attack by slaters and slugs by placing some kind of collar around the plant. The plant can still easily obtain sunlight and air.

What you do

❋ Cut away the bottom of your bottle.

❋ Remove the cap and carefully press the bottle into the ground or mulch surrounding your plant.

Figure 25. Seedling protectors.

❋ Alternatively, cut away the neck and base of the bottle and insert the main body into the ground.

19

SOLAR STILL

This is a great project for young people during the summer time. It demonstrates the principles of a solar still and it really works! You won't get heaps of fresh water but you will obtain some.

What you do

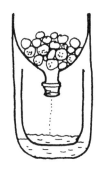

Figure 26. Using a solar still to collect fresh water.

❋ Cut the top off a 2l plastic bottle. Both parts are used.

❋ Cut a 1.5l cool drink bottle in half. Only the bottom part is used. The top part can be kept for a funnel.

❋ Pour 100ml of impure muddy or salty water into the base of the large bottle.

❋ Place the bottom part of the smaller bottle inside the other.

❋ Lower the top part of the large bottle (inverted) with the screw cap on, into the body of its base and gently push in to hold it against the wall.

❋ Place some stones or marbles in the neck part to help keep the neck in place. Leave the still in the sunlight for a day and examine to see how much water you have collected.

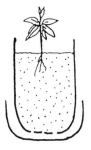
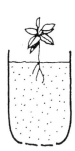

Figure 27. Flower pots and water dish.

FLOWER POTS

You never seem to have enough flower pots to germinate your seeds and to transplant young seedlings from the seedling tray.

Additional materials for this project

❋ 6mm drill bit and drill.

20

What you do

✽ Cut away the neck and top half of the cool drink bottle.

✽ Drill about 6 x 6mm diameter holes, randomly placed, in the base so that water can drain away.

✽ Cut away the base from another bottle. This is for the dish under the pot.

✽ Fill your pot with soil and sow your seeds!

From A Permaculture Perspective

Many of the projects in this activity deal with pest control. Controlling pests and disease in your garden will enhance the quantity and quality of your produce. Permaculture is about maximising diversity, creating an abundance of good, healthy food and designing energy-efficient, intensive systems that are ecologically sustainable.

Recycling is an important consideration for all individuals and communities. We all have a responsibility to reduce our consumption, re-use as much as possible and then finally recycle.

Many common household items can be recycled. Besides plastic bottles (as we have just seen), glass, metals and paper are easy to recycle. Many local authorities now provide bins for household recyclable items, and many community-based organisations offer depots as well.

Newspaper Pots

These biodegradable pots are great for fast germinating seeds or transferring seedlings from trays. You use newspaper sheeting to make tube stock pots. When the seedlings are ready you plant the whole pot!

What you need

❉ Newspaper.

❉ Potting mixture for seedlings. Make an equal mixture of coarse sand and peat or perlite, or some other combination of these three.

❉ Scissors.

❉ Ice cream container, flower pot or 2l soft drink bottle.

What you do

❉ Take one sheet of newspaper folded in half. For pots 12cm tall, fold and crease the paper in three equal sections. To make pots 9cm tall, fold the paper in half and then half again. You end up with four equal sections.

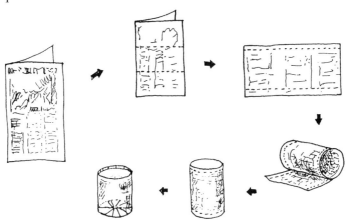

Figure 28. Making newspaper strip pots.

* Cut along the creases and on the end crease so you now have six or eight strips.

* Roll each strip into a cylinder about 5 cm in diameter and fold over a 1 cm strip at one end. This strengthens the top of the pot.

* Fold a 2 cm strip at the bottom and tuck it in so that a base is formed. Alternatively, pinch and fold the bottom, staple to seal and flatten the pot as best you can.

Figure 29. Use funnel to fill each pot with soil and plant.

* Stand the cylinders in a 2l ice cream container, flower pot or the base of a 2l soft or cool drink container.

* Use a funnel (from the soft drink bottle activity) to fill each pot with potting mix. Tall potting tubes are ideal for beans and corn, while smaller ones are suitable for tomatoes and lettuce. A wide pot (8 cm) can be used for pumpkins. By custom fitting the pots to the plants you conserve potting soil.

* Plant two or three seeds into each pot. If you are transferring seedlings from propagation trays use a knife to make a deep hole in the centre of the soil in the pot.

  Carefully remove the seedling from the tray and direct the plant roots into the hole. Be careful not to damage the sensitive roots. Back-fill the roots with the soil.

* When it is time to plant the pots you might like to prise open the base of the pot. The root structure should be sufficient to hold the soil in place. Lower the pot into a hole in your garden bed. If you leave the top of the pot about 2 cm above ground level you might give your young seedlings some protection from cut worms.

Organic Pest Control

When we first started in permaculture we made many different types of organic sprays to deter pests. While we had great success, we felt that even this is probably unnecessary. If you have lots of strategies for pest control the need for sprays diminishes. We haven't used any sprays for the last four years.

Integrated pest management is a method of pest control where many strategies are used. For example, you could use:

❉ Animal predators such as frogs for caterpillars, predatory wasps for small insects, and ducks for snails and slugs.

❉ Mixed planting in orchards and gardens to encourage predatory species. For example, buckwheat attracts hoverflies. These beneficial insects prey on aphids, leafhoppers and mealy bugs.

❉ Herbs and other plants in companion planting.

❉ Sound management and husbandry to discourage soil and leaf pests.

❉ Plant competition to control land and aquatic weeds.

❉ Insect traps and behavioural chemicals.

❉ Mechanical management and barriers, such as the handpicking of insects and snails, sticky/wet bases (using Vaseline) of fruit trees to discourage climbing insects, and sawdust around garden beds to discourage slugs and snails.

❉ Specific biological pest control, such as fungus or bacteria to kill pests.

❉ Attractants/food to induce predators into garden.

❉ Crop rotation. By moving the area where you grow tomatoes, potatoes and other vegetables around each year you minimise the spread of disease. The cycle of pest and disease organisms is broken.

Crop rotation also has the added benefits of nutrient and fertiliser balance Some vegetables, such as leaf and fruit crops, may prefer high levels of nitrogen, potassium and phosphorous and thus respond to the addition of animal manures.

Root crops do not grow well in animal manures and heavy mulch. Consequently, they become stunted or distorted. By rotating these types of crops there is a greater efficiency of fertiliser use.

One example of a crop rotation system is to plant legumes such as peas and beans in the first year then in subsequent years leaf flower vegetables such as brassicas (cauliflower and broccoli) and silverbeet, then fruit crops such as tomatoes and capsicum and finally root crops which include carrots, beetroot and onions. Some organic growers then leave this area fallow for a year to 'rest' the soil.

Should you have to use sprays to control pests or outbreaks of disease, here are some useful ones to make:

SELF-INSECT SPRAY
Use a teaspoonful of the insect pest and mash it up in a cup of water. Stand this in the sun for a day, filter through an old stocking and mix with 4l of water. Said to be pathogenically potent for the insect pest. This even works for woodlice and millipedes.

GARLIC SPRAY
Finely chop up 4 garlic cloves. Add this to one litre of water and let it stand overnight. Grate some soap flakes (about a level tablespoon) into the mixture. This helps the spray to stick to the leaves. Garlic spray is a good general purpose insecticide.

One variation is to include a couple of hot chillies or onions. Some people blend the garlic cloves in one cup of paraffin oil and let this stand for a day or two before soap is added.

FRUIT FLY CONTROL
To one litre of water add 10ml ammonia solution or urine, 10ml vanilla essence and 100g sugar (or 2 tablespoons honey). Partly fill small jars or the fruit fly traps made from plastic soft drink bottles (see page 14)

and suspend 3 or 4 in each tree. The bottles must be kept clean to have any effect.

Many commercial organic producers use a substance called protein hydrolysate which is like marmite or vegemite in smell and appearance. The substance is diluted and then placed in the traps.

Some research has been undertaken on the use of neem oil, which is sprayed onto fruit, for fruit fly control. Neem oil only repels the fly, but initial experimental results indicate it may be just as successful as the protein hydrolysate. Neem oil is only now becoming available for general use, so you may need to ask around for a supply.

WORMWOOD SPRAY
Add 15g of dried leaves to 1l of water. Simmer for 30 minutes and allow to cool slowly. Use only on mature plants for larger pests such as caterpillars, moths and aphids.

PYRETHRUM
This is a natural insecticide which paralyses insects. It can be used in dry powder form or a spray made by mixing 30g of dry flower heads and 50ml of methylated spirits.

Figure 30. Hiding your vegetables amongst herbs and other plants helps to protect them. Spraying, even with organic substances, is a last resort.

Grind the young flower heads to make a fine powder. You can either use this powder directly on your vegetables or make a stock solution by adding methylated spirits.

Keep this stock solution in a dark coloured bottle or jar which has an airtight lid, as sunlight will initiate the breakdown of the pyrethrum. Pyrethrum is toxic but it deactivates in bright light. Dilute this stock twenty times with water when you want to use it. You should apply the powder or solution at night as it will also kill beneficial insects such as bees.

CHAMOMILE TEA

This is effective against damping-off in cold, damp places, and mildew on fruit trees. Use a handful of fresh flowers or 30ml of dried flowers in one litre of boiling water. Cover and steep for 15 minutes, strain and use immediately as a spray. You can also add a small amount of seaweed to the chamomile to make a more potent antifungal spray.

RHUBARB SPRAY

One kilogram of leaves in 2l of water simmered for 30 minutes makes an effective spray against small insects such as aphids and whitefly. Rhubarb leaves contain oxalic acid, which is quite toxic, so use this spray at night time.

From A Permaculture Perspective

Permaculture is a holistic approach to sustainable living. It integrates many disciplines such as agriculture, economics, and wilderness management, all of which are important considerations in pest management.

One of the principles of permaculture is to increase the sum of the yields. This is accomplished by examining the total yield of the permaculture-designed system which is provided by animals, annuals, perennials, trees and crops. The total yield increases dramatically when pests and diseases are controlled.

Pest and diseases only occur when there is an imbalance in the natural cycles involving predators and prey – essentially this means that there are not enough predators to control the pests.

Sheet Mulching

Sheet mulching allows you to build simple, low maintenance, no-dig garden beds ideal for your annual vegetables and herbs. Larger shrubs and trees should be planted directly into the soil and spot mulched (see page 36). Warning, some plants cannot survive in rich sources of mulch, so this technique is not suitable for them. What is placed in each layer varies depending on what is available. For example, you might have access to seaweed, or you might have to be content with plant prunings.

What you need

✤ Newspaper, carpet, underfelt or cardboard.

✤ Waterholding wheelbarrow, 200l drum or large container.

✤ Selection of green plant materials such as lucerne hay bales, weeds, prunings or lawn clippings.

✤ Compost – either self-made or bought.

✤ One bale of straw, forest floor mulch or some other shredded plants or mulch for top layer.

✤ Bag of blood and bone or animal manure such as cow, chicken, pig or sheep.

✤ Bag of rock dust (optional, but recommended).

✤ Reticulation hose and fittings (optional).

What you do

✤ There is no need to dig or prepare the soil. You can build your garden bed directly over lawn or weeds. You may have to slash the weeds or mow the lawn, but leave the trimmings and cut plant material where they fall.

* Soak the newspaper or cardboard pieces in a wheelbarrow or 200l (44gal) drum, which is tilted on its side so you can remove the wet paper easily. You can soak the newspaper overnight if you want to prepare for the next day, but generally this length of soaking is not necessary for most garden beds.

* Sprinkle blood and bone or chicken manure at a rate of one handful per square metre over the bed or lawn area. This helps to quickly break down the organic material and make it available to worms and growing plants. If your soil is of poor quality, you can add some rock dust as well. Water the manure in for a minute or two.

* Cover the entire garden area with overlapping layers of newspaper (or cardboard). Use 10 - 12 sheets thick and place them so that about 20% of the newspaper sheets overlaps the previous layer. It is easiest to lay the paper sheets in one direction.

  Carpet or underfelt can be used instead of newspaper. There is no need to initially soak these. Make sure that you do not use rubber-backed carpet, which does not break down in the soil. If you are building a garden on top of couch or other invasive grass make this layer thicker and overlap well. This layer protects the soil underneath, encourages earthworms and soil animals into the area and prevents the germination of weed seeds.

Straw or mulch
Compost
Green material and animal manure
Newspaper
Slashed plant material

Figure 31. Section through a typical sheet mulched bed.

✽ Add a layer of green material such as lucerne hay or shredded plant material. This green manure layer could be about 15 - 20cm thick.

✽ Add a couple of shovelfuls of animal manure per square metre of garden and water this in for a minute. Generally, add one and a halftimes more cow, sheep or horse manure than chicken or pig. The plant-animal manure layer will slowly break down into a slow, cold compost and provide nutrients for your plants once they have become established.

✽ Add a 20 - 25cm layer of compost. You can use some combination of compost with soil or organic soil mix. Some compost mulches such as mushroom mix are very alkaline while others are fresh and 'steaming' but what you need is aged compost.

Add some more rock dust -about one handful for every square metre. This provides both essential and trace elements which are necessary for plant development.

All too often plants grow very fast and then don't produce the amount of food we would expect. A correct balance of all nutrients is very important.

It is in this layer that you plant your seedlings or seeds.

If you intend to drip irrigate the garden bed, place your hose material in now. Soaker hose material, is the most economic and water-efficient method of reticulation. Avoid sprays and sprinklers.

✽ Cap the garden bed with a 5cm layer of straw or shredded street prunings (sometimes called forest mulch). Do not use hay – it contains seeds which will germinate and cause problems. To eliminate this problem place the hay, and even straw, in the chicken run for a few days. They will remove all the seeds. Rake up the straw/hay when you need to.

This top layer keeps the garden bed cool, prevents excess water loss by evaporation and protects the earthworms and microbes that are essential to your garden.

❋ Carefully spread the straw or mulch to one side, dig a hole in the compost and plant your seedlings or seeds.

If you are putting in larger herbs and vegetables you can plant them before you add the final mulch layer.

Circle Garden Beds

Circle garden beds are usually only about 1 - 2m in diameter. They are the most compact and useful of all gardens. Two types of circle garden beds are described below. Each has its own merits and combinations of these are common in many gardens.

CIRCLE GARDEN BED 1

What you do

❋ Build the standard sheet mulched garden bed in a circle about one metre in diameter.

❋ Plant a range of vegetables with their companion herbs to create functional guilds. A guild is a collection of plants (and animals) that support and enhance each other. Often this type of planning and planting is used for pest control. In many cases, the particular plants benefit each other by the natural chemicals they exude into the soil which promote growth and prevent disease.

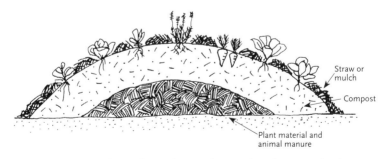
Straw or mulch
Compost
Plant material and animal manure

Figure 32. Section through Circle Garden Bed 1, showing the layers and companion planted herbs and vegetables.

31

Food scraps
and other organic
material
↓

Figure 33. Mounded Circle Garden Bed 2 with a central food scrap area.

CIRCLE GARDEN BED 2 – MOUNDED

What you do

❁ Before the sheet mulching technique is used, scrape or dig out a small hole in the middle of where your circle garden bed will be.

❁ Mound this soil around the perimeter of the bed.

❁ Build the mulch layers as usual, but add more animal manure, compost or food scraps to the middle section. This will provide lots of nutrients for the growing plants. This middle section can be topped up whenever you feel your plants need a little extra feed.

❁ If you are planning to grow climbing plants such as peas and beans, make a circular support and place this in the middle section.

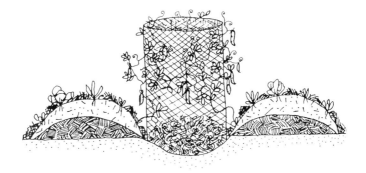

Figure 34. Chicken wire middle section support for climbing plants.

Mandala Garden

A mandala garden is based on a circular shape. By marking out a pattern on top of the soil you can create either a keyhole garden bed (mandala) or a circle garden bed sequence which has pathways between. Garden beds with keyhole paths provide more growing edge and allow you to step into the garden and easily access all plants.

What you need

❉ A piece of string 5.4m long. Tie the ends together and tie a knot 1.8m either side. You end up with three knots which are 1.8m apart.

❉ A piece of string one metre long. Tie the ends together.

❉ 7 wooden or metal rod stakes.

❉ 1m^3 of green plant material (green manure).

❉ 2 wheelbarrows of animal manure.

❉ 2m^3 of compost.

❉ 1 bale of straw or half a metre of plant prunings mulch.

❉ 1m^3 of material for paths – sawdust, leaves or street prunings. Choose material that doesn't break down too rapidly (even pine needles).

What you do

❉ The mandala garden is about 6m^2. Place a stake in the middle of where the garden is going to be built.

❉ Identify where the path that enters the garden is to be placed.

❉ Using the long string line wrapped around the centre stake with one knot on the stake, measure and place a second stake 1.8m (one knot away) from the centre and about 0.5m from the path entrance.

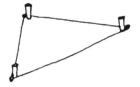

Figure 35. Making a triangle shape with the string and stakes.

❀ With the string now wrapped around the two stakes, each with a knot alongside, stretch the string to make a third position and insert a stake where the third knot is. You should have three stakes 1.8 metres apart from each other in a triangle shape.

❀ Lift the string off one stake (never the centre one), move the string around to where the next position should be and repeat the previous instructions.

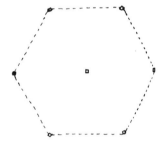

❀ Continue to move the string off one stake and use the other two to find the position of the next stake. You end up with six stakes around one central one.

Figure 36. A hexagon shape made with string and stakes.

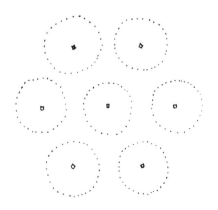

Figure 37. Circle garden layout.

❀ Use the shorter piece of string, placed over each stake, to scribe a 1m diameter circle around each stake. Another stake or piece of wood or wire can be used. You can use this garden layout if you want a series of circle gardens with equidistant paths between as shown below. The pathways should be no more than 0.8m wide.

❀ For the mandala garden, link one circle to another by drawing symmetrical curves from each circle top and middle as shown in figure 38. The centre circle is used for a bed, a seating area, a tyre pond, a deciduous tree to give filtered shade in summer, a sundial or birdbath.

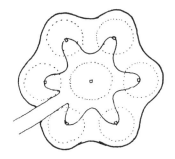

Figure 38. Converting the circle garden into a mandala shape.

✽ Completely sheet mulch this bed and plant out as shown in figure 39. Leave an entrance or exit path, having two can be beneficial when you need to walk via this garden to other areas.

✽ Fill in between the mandala garden bed or circle gardens with material for the paths. Sawdust, pine needles, leaves, shredded mulch or street prunings are all suitable.

Figure 39. Planted mandala garden.

A DOUBLE MANDALA

This should be about 9m², with beds up to one and a half metres across (*see figure 40*). This type of garden is ideal for school children because students can access both sides of the garden beds. For this reason, the central circle garden should be less than 2m in diameter. This bed could become a stock garden for herbs or flowers.

Figure 40. A planted double mandala shaped garden.

Planting Trees

Large perennial shrubs and trees can be planted directly into the ground and spot mulched in a garden bed. Spot mulching is used for individual trees and provides protection to the plant.

What you need

✽ Spade or shovel.

Figure 41. Planted and mulched tree.

✽ Bucket of forest mulch, street prunings or biscuit of straw (usually a layer about 8cm thick).

✽ Two buckets of compost, or worm castings, and animal manure mixture.

✽ Gypsum (optional for clay soils).

✽ Bentonite clay (optional for sandy soils).

✽ Rock dust (optional for poor quality soils).

What you do

✽ Dig a hole twice the diameter and depth of the plant pot.

✽ If you have clay soil add a handful of gypsum to the hole. Gypsum makes the clay particles clump together and this improves drainage, and water and root penetration.

✽ If you have a sandy soil add a handful of bentonite clay. This improves the water holding capacity of the soil.

✽ If you have poor quality soil, such as mainly sand and little organic matter add a handful of rock dust. Important elements are slowly released to plants.

- Add one bucket of compost and animal manure.
- Remove the plant from the pot and place it immediately in the compost in the hole. You must plant trees quickly because long delays will dehydrate the roots and damage the plant.
- Add the rest of the compost mixture to fill the hole.
- Water the plant in.
- Place a 5cm layer of prunings, mulch or straw around the tree. Do not cover the stem of the tree as fungus/other diseases may affect it.

From A Permaculture Perspective

Production increases with the amount of edge or growing surface area. The use of sheet mulching, keyhole garden beds, circle gardens and compost heaps all improve the efficiency of the system and save energy, water and maintenance time. Soil fertility can be improved by the use of mulches, manures, green manure crops and other types of organic matter. We have the responsibility to care for the Earth and this includes the soil, the organisms that live in the soil and rehabilitating damaged and marginal sites. Erosion and soil degradation are halted when we cover the soil and increase its organic content and biological activity. Water retention by the soil, and water availability to the plants increases, and healthy soil means healthy plants and healthy food.

Sheet mulching is a great way to get you started on the road to growing your own food. It enables your plants to grow without the competition from weeds (or pioneers as we like to call them), and the compost layers provide an abundance of the necessary nutrients for healthy plants. Sheet mulching is also great when you have a patch of grass or weeds that you want to replace with a vegetable garden.

However, there are other ways to grow plants. Plants grow best in soil, and treating your soil so that it contains a wide range of nutrients will enable shrubs to be placed directly into the ground. You may get a flourish of weeds until your herbs and vegetables are large enough to shade them out.

Making Compost

Compost is essential for every garden – and it is so easy to make, provided you do it properly. To make good compost there are five conditions:

1. *A mixture of plant and animal material.* You can make compost from plant material alone but it does take a long time. Adding animal manure produces a high source of nitrogen which is used up by the bacteria and other organisms which make compost.

   The carbon-nitrogen ratio is an important aspect of decomposition – a satisfactory ratio is something like 20:1. This means that there are twenty parts of carbon to one part of nitrogen in the organic material. This kind of ratio is achieved when you have a mixture of plant and animal material as described in the method that follows.

2. *Size of material.* The smaller the particles the faster the decomposition. This is because the smaller particles have a greater surface area on which the bacteria can act. Putting prunings through a mulcher or chopping them up as small as possible will help the decomposition process.

3. *Oxygen.* Decomposition without oxygen will cause the heap to smell and go sour. It will also encourage flies and other insects which will breed in it. To make sure your heap has lots of oxygen you will have to drive a wooden garden stake into the heap to allow oxygen to penetrate to all parts of the material. Turning the compost heap each week will also aerate the decomposing material.

4. *Water.* As a general rule, the amount of water you will need to add to the heap is about 50% of the heap size. The plant and animal mixture should be like a damp sponge – thoroughly wet but not dripping!

   Most compost heaps that do not work properly are due to lack of water. Because the heap tends to dry out, especially in the warmer weather, you may have to add water occasionally.

5. *Temperature.* If the compost mix has been done properly you can expect that the heap will increase in temperature to about 55 - 60°C within a few days. If after three days the heap is not quite hot in the centre, something is wrong. Certain bacteria live and work at this temperature and they cause the start of the decomposition process. Within a few more days the temperature starts to drop. Other types of bacteria now continue to make the compost. After a week or two the compost is much colder, but bacteria and other organisms, such as worms, are still hard at work.

The following description is one way to make compost and additional variations are included for those who want to do something a little different.

What you need

❋ 1m³ of green material, such as shredded weeds and prunings.

❋ 40kg (large bag) of animal manure such as chicken, cow, sheep or pig – a combination of any of these is all right.

❋ Access to water.

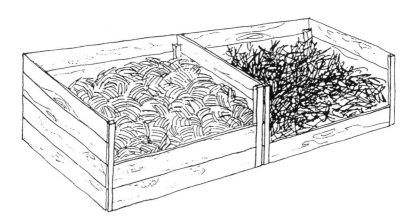

Figure 42. An easy to make two bay compost bin. Composting material can be turned from one bay to another or they can be used seperately.

- ❊ Pitch-fork, shovel and a wooden garden stake or pole.

- ❊ Covering material such as black plastic sheeting, carpet, underfelt or even sheets of corrugated iron.

- ❊ Optional: some wood ash, dolomite, crushed limestone, rock dust, compost activator herbs such as yarrow and comfrey leaves, urine.

What you do

- ❊ Place a layer about 30cm thick and 2m diameter of green plant material on the soil or pit area.

- ❊ Spread three shovelfuls of animal manure on top.

- ❊ Use a pitch fork to mix the plant and animal material.

- ❊ Water the mixture well. It should end up like a damp sponge.

- ❊ There are a few optional strategies you can employ to make good compost. When materials decompose they create acidic conditions. You can usually tell when this has happened because the heap will smell and you will see lots of flying insects around the pile.

Break up prunings as much as possible

Figure 43. Making a large round compost heap.

Acidic conditions can be overcome by the addition of crushed limestone, wood ash (from the stove fire) or dolomite (which is a mixture of calcium and magnesium carbonates). Add half a shovelful to each layer you build.

Rock dust can also be added to improve the quality of the compost. The addition of one shovelful per layer will provide a greater amount of minerals for your plants.

To activate your compost heap add a few sprigs or leaves of yarrow or comfrey. Alternatively, 1l of urine is a good compost activator.

* Place another layer of plant material and animal manure on top. Mix and water in again. Repeat until you have 3 or 4 layers – up to one and a half metres high.

* Use a wooden stake or pole to drive holes into the heap. Do this about a dozen times.

* Cover the heap with plastic sheeting, sheets of tin, carpet or underfelt. This keeps the heap warm and speeds decomposition. It also prevents excess water loss.

Figure 44. Punching holes and turning increase air circulation in the heap.

✤ After one week remove the protective covering and turn the heap inside out with a pitch fork. The top should become the bottom and the bottom, inner part of the original heap becomes spread over the top of the new heap.

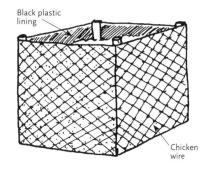

Figure 45. A simple chicken wire compost bin.

✤ The more your turn the heap the faster compost is made. Repeat the turning process each week for about four weeks. Drain coil (sub-soil drainage pipe) laid at the bottom of the heap will help aerate it and the coil could save you the chore of frequently turning the compost heap. When the compost has a nice earthy smell it is ready for the garden.

From A Permaculture Perspective

No organic matter should leave your property. For you, the days of leaving your prunings on the road verge for the local council to pick up are over. All of this organic matter should be composted, buried in trash lines or pits, or fed to your earthworms.

Composting is nature's way of ensuring that matter is recycled. When an organism dies it decays and decomposes. Bacteria, fungi and many other soil organisms break down the tissues and organic material of the dead organism. These nutrients, essential for plant growth, are released into the soil and then become available to plants or other creatures that need them for their survival. Anything that poultry won't or don't eat, such as broccoli stalks, carrots and tea bags, can be fed to earthworms or placed in the compost heap.

We should be using everything at its optimum level and recycling all wastes. Food and garden wastes, which generally make up 30 - 55% of domestic landfill disposal, can be recycled via the compost heap to produce humus, which is rich in nutrients, holds water and makes plants grow.

Natural Liquid Fertilisers

Natural organic fertilisers are the best for your plants and soil. Generally, you should fertilise your soil when it is moist, when plants are transpiring and actively taking up nutrients and water.

Foliar sprays are very useful. They should be applied, if possible, to the underside of leaves during the late afternoon or evening when high humidity triggers the stomata to open and so absorb the nutrients in the spray. Besides the root system, plants can absorb nutrients through their leaves, stems and even flowers.

Commercial foliates (leaf sprays) are available and you should purchase seaweed or fishmeal products. However, you can easily make your own as described in some of the recipes below.

What you need

✿ Fermentation bin, or plastic or steel drum.

✿ Old stocking, gauze or cloth.

✿ Hot and cold water.

✿ A variety of plant leaves or animal manure (depending on the chosen recipe).

✿ Non-sealing lid or hessian bag for the bucket.

Figure 46. Making bulk liquid fertiliser in a 200l (44 gal) drum by suspending a bag of manure in the water.

Comfrey

Comfrey is rich in potassium. It is a deep rooted herb which draws up lots of different nutrients, such as iron, magnesium and calcium from the soil.

43

What you do

❀ Half fill a fermentation bin or some other container with large mature leaves. Tear the leaves into small pieces.

❀ Add 1l of boiling water and leave for five minutes. Hot water dissolves the waxy coating on plant tissues and thus speeds the initial breakdown of the plants.

❀ Fill the bin with cold water from the tap.

❀ Cover with a hessian bag or lid – but don't seal the bin as gases need to escape during the decomposition process. Because these liquid fertilisers tend to smell, it is best to place them far from the house!

❀ Leave to ferment for a couple of weeks.

❀ Strain the broth through an old stocking or piece of gauze if you want a foliar spray. Dilute 10:1 before applying to the plant foliage. Remaining solids can be added to the worm farm or compost heap.

❀ Dilute 2 or 3 times before use if you are just adding the brew to the soil.

Seaweed

Seaweed is rich in elements such as bromine and iodine, and also contains high levels of nitrogen, sodium, iron, magnesium and calcium. You can buy bagged seaweed in some nurseries which can then be used for this recipe.

What you do

❀ Wash off any excess sand or salt from your seaweed.

❀ Half fill a fermentation bin with chopped-up seaweed. A mixture of different coloured seaweed will provide a range of nutrients. Kelp (brown) and sea grasses (green) are very common along the coast.

44

❊ Top up the bin with cold water.

❊ Cover the bin and let the seaweed ferment for a month or more.

❊ Strain through a stocking or gauze and dilute 20 times before use. Remaining solids can be placed in the worm farm or compost heap.

All Purpose Herb Fertiliser

This recipe is a mixture of several herbs. It will provide a wide range of essential elements for plant growth.

Stinging nettles contain sodium, sulphur, nitrogen, calcium, potassium, iron and copper.

Chamomile contains high levels of calcium, potassium and phosphorus.

Yarrow contains copper, nitrogen, potassium and phosphorus, while comfrey has potassium, nitrogen, calcium, magnesium and iron.

What you do

❊ Use stinging nettles, chamomile, yarrow and comfrey. Chop up and half fill the bucket.

❊ Add any of the following for a greater range of nutrients: 1l human urine, or ¼ of a bucket of weeds or lawn clippings. You could also add any of these herbs – dill (sulphur and iron), dandelion (copper), tansy (potassium) or horsetail (silica).

❊ Add 1l of boiling water. Leave for five minutes.

❊ Fill with cold water and allow to ferment for a few weeks. Cover the bucket.

❊ Strain if you want a foliar spray. Dilute this ten times with water.

❊ Dilute 3 or 4 times if you are adding this liquid fertiliser to the soil.

Poultry Manure

Chicken manure is high in nitrogen and phosphorus. It is quite strong and so it must be diluted with water before using it on your plants.

What you do

❉ Half fill a fermentation bin with manure.

❉ Fill the bin with cold water.

❉ Cover the bin and leave for a couple of weeks.

❉ Dilute ten times or more when you require some for the garden.

❉ Strain through the stocking or cloth if you want a foliar spray.

❉ For larger volumes of fertiliser, half fill an old hessian bag with manure, and then suspend it in 200l (44 gal) drum filled with water (*see figure 46 on page 43*). Leave for a few weeks and then use.

Worm Castings

Worm castings are produced when earthworms pass through the soil and digest food. It is essentially worm poo. Worm castings, which can be harvested from your earthworm farm or bought from most nurseries, are soluble in water and make an excellent fertiliser.

What you do

❉ Add 1kg of worm castings to the laundry bucket.

❉ Fill the bucket with water and stir for a few minutes. Leave it for ten minutes and then stir again.

❉ Allow to settle for a further five minutes and then carefully pour off the liquid into another container. The liquid should be dark brown in colour. Any residual solids can be placed directly onto the garden.

❧ Dilute 5 times before applying to the soil or leaves. Filter the liquid if you want a foliar spray.

From A Permaculture Perspective

Permaculture-designed gardens need management and maintenance. Managing resources such as our crops, vegetables and mulch are essential if we want to recycle energy on site and develop a sustainable system. If systems are not managed and cared for, some of our biological resources become lost, destructive or out of control.

Garden maintenance is one part of the overall management of the system. We can improve the quality of the soil by maintaining high levels of organic matter in the form of manures, fertilisers and mulch. Liquid fertilisers provide nutrients which are readily available to plants. They are easy to make and they don't kill or damage earthworms and soil organisms, unlike chemical fertilisers.

Earthworm Farm

There are earthworms and then there are earthworms! The most common earthworms which you can buy are red wrigglers and tiger worms. These are really manure worms – they prefer high amounts of animal wastes and they are generally surface feeders.

Manure worms are not usually introduced into the garden or paddocks. Conditions in these areas rarely suit the redworms and tigerworms, which are very sensitive to harsh conditions. Sure, many survive, and if you do want to introduce them into the garden it is best to do so as egg capsules. When the eggs hatch and small worms emerge, they tend to stay in the garden, near where they were born.

True earthworms, those that till and aerate the soil and digest organic matter are often hard to find and certainly harder to buy. From a permaculture point of view, the earthworm farm should be placed close to the vegetable gardens and chicken run.

Normally, any food scraps go to the chickens first and once they have had what they want out, the rest is raked up and given to the earthworms. Chickens don't eat such things as tea bags, citrus peel, broccoli stalks, carrots and onion skins, but earthworms will devour anything organic. However, don't give them too much of any one thing – they certainly wouldn't like a bucketful of lemon peel! An earthworm farm, therefore, should be placed in Zone 2.

If you don't have chickens or other poultry then your earthworms can be kept much closer to the house in Zone 1 (see page 66 for a description of Zones).

Mini-farm

The mini-farm is ideal for domestic use. If you live in a rental house or a block of flats or units, and don't have chickens or other poultry, then a small earthworm farm, which will generally service your needs and consume organic food wastes, is all that you need.

What you need

❉ Cardboard box, polystyrene, foam box, or half a 200l drum – any of these with a lid. You could even use an old laundry trough, bath tub or cut-down rainwater tank. Make sure that there are drainage holes as earthworms cannot swim!

❉ Shredded newspaper.

❉ Animal manure – horse, pig, sheep or cow.

❉ Earthworms – red wrigglers (*Lumbricus rubellus*) and tiger worms (*Eisenia fetida*).

❉ 2 bricks or pieces of similar diameter timber logs.

What you do

❉ Punch holes in the bottom of your container so that excess water can drain away and air can enter the farm. Use a drill, nail punch or knife to make about 12 holes evenly spaced over the base of the container. If using a cardboard box you may want to line it with a plastic garbage bag – the earthworms would eventually eat the cardboard.

❉ The bedding material is a mixture of wet, shredded newspaper and animal manure (50:50). It should have a moisture content like a damp sponge. The depth of this material should not be more than 30cm. Remember that these types of worms are surface feeders, but they do need a place deeper down to retreat to in very hot weather.

❉ Start off with about 1,000 worms or half a kilo. Many nurseries sell the right quantities and types of worms.

❉ If you only have kitchen scraps to get rid of allow about $0.15m^2$ of box surface area per person in the household. This equates to about 5kg of organic garbage disposal each week. So, if you have four people in your household, the size of the farm box should be at least $0.6m^2$ or a box about 80 x $80cm^2$.

49

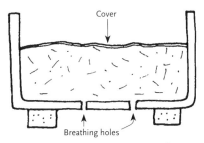

Cover

Breathing holes

Figure 47. Mini-earthworm farm.

❈ The best system is to have two boxes and feed the worms alternately. Generally, 2kg of worms can devour 1kg (and often more) of food scraps every day. Earthworms can ingest up to their own body weight every day, but they cannot convert this amount of matter efficiently.

❈ Support your mini-farm on a couple of bricks or piece of timber. It is important to raise the farm off the ground to allow air circulation and water drainage and to prevent your worms from leaving the box – they don't like dangling in mid air!

❈ Place a dish underneath your farm to collect any water that seeps through. This liquid is an excellent fertiliser. Dilute ten times and apply the solution to your garden plants. Alternatively, collect some of the vermicompost and make a liquid fertiliser. See the activity on *Natural Liquid Fertilisers* earlier in this book for instructions.

❈ Harvesting your worms or the worm poo (castings and vermicompost) is discussed at the end of this section (*Large Scale Earthworm Farm*).

Ben Hur Model

This earthworm farm is called the Ben Hur model because the earthworms start at one part of the farm and slowly move around and around it – like the famous race of long ago.

You can build the farm directly on the soil but if you wish to harvest the vermicompost it will be easier if it is built on a thin concrete base. Slope the concrete floor from the inner walls to the outer walls to allow drainage of excess rainwater.

One advantage of this earthworm farm model is that you can disassemble the farm and move it to another location. The concrete slabs are held together loosely by metal channels.

What you need

❀ 16 concrete slabs, 600 x 600mm.

❀ 4 timber sleepers (each 2.1m).

❀ 4 x 2.4m 'U' channel, 40mm wide and 25mm sides.

❀ 2 x 2.4m corner mould.

❀ Pop rivets and gun.

What you do

❀ Place 4 slabs upright in a square around a deciduous tree such as a stone fruit, pear or apple. Keep the slabs together by placing a 60cm length of corner mould, or angle iron, partly buried, on each corner. The deciduous tree will shade the farm in summer and allow warm sunlight in during winter.

❀ Place other slabs around this in a square 3 slabs wide. The distance between the inside slabs and the outer slabs is 60cm. Rivet together 2 pieces of 60cm long channel to join each slab pair (*as shown in figure 48*). Use corner mould again to hold the corners in.

❀ Half bury the sleepers at the bottom of the outside square.

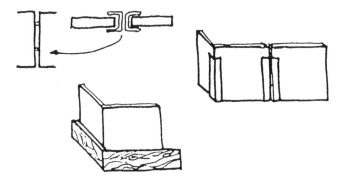

Figure 48. Joint details used to build the Ben Hur model of worm farm.

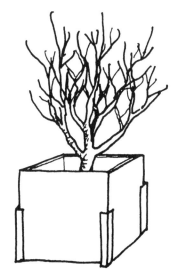

Figure 49. Centre slabs around tree.

✤ Rake the ground between the inner slabs and the outer slabs and add a thin layer of concrete, slightly sloping towards the outside, to drain excess water away. Place flat sheet metal lids over the slabs to cover the earthworm farm. Even old corrugated iron roofing would be suitable.

✤ If you have the time and inclination you can build a timber frame or metal channel frame to hinge the lids. This does make it easier to service the farm.

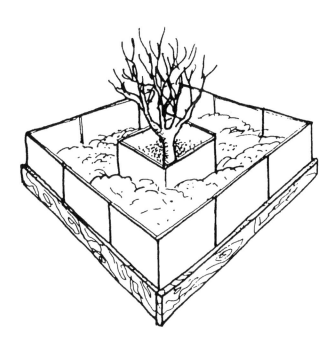

Figure 50. The finished Ben Hur earthworm farm, shown minus the roofing.

Large Scale Worm Farm

This worm farm system is more appropriate on a larger property where you have the room and facilities for greater worm production – to the extent that you could start a small business operation to breed and sell worms.

What you need

* Timber sleepers.

* 15cm nails.

* Corrugated iron sheeting.

* Bedding material.

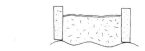

Figure 51. A large scale earthworm farm.

* Second-hand carpet or underfelt, or black plastic sheeting.

What you do

* The sleepers are used as walls for long beds. Make the earthworm farm beds about 1m across and whatever length you like. Cut one of the sleepers in half to make the two ends. Use nails to secure the sleeper ends to the edges of the sides – to form a box. For long beds drive nails in at an angle to tie sleepers together.

* You have a choice about whether you want worms to be on the ground or not. You will lose quite a few worms if you place the farm directly on the surface of the ground – but this may not matter if they go into your garden areas. To contain your worms you will need to raise the farm off the ground. Simply lay overlapping old corrugated iron sheeting on the ground and put your sleeper box on top. The corrugations will enable excess water to drain away without drowning your worms and generally contain the worms in the worm farm.

* Fill the sleeper box with organic material – horse manure, shredded paper, lawn clippings (not fresh), weeds and so on. The depth of the material only has to be the height of a sleeper, about 25cm high.

53

- Make sure that the bedding and food materials are moist – put the sprinklers on or hand-water.

- Introduce your worms. You will need several thousand to start with. If they have good living and breeding conditions, then after one year you could expect to have one million worms.

- Cover your earthworm farm with old carpet, hessian or underfelt to keep it from drying out. Black plastic sheeting is all right to use in the winter but not for the summer time. Remember to periodically check that the beds are moist and there is ample food.

- Harvest the worms or castings by removing the cover during the daytime. Worms do not like the light and will retreat further down. Scoop off a 25mm layer of the castings or vermicompost. Leave the farm exposed to the sun for another ten minutes. Scoop another layer of casings off and keep repeating these steps until you have all the material you want or all you have left is a bundle of worms.

From A Permaculture Perspective

Earthworms are good for soils. They are nature's cultivators and they increase soil fertility by breaking down organic material, making nutrients more available to plants and allowing better penetration of plant roots, water and oxygen into soils.

In every ecosystem on the earth, animals, such as earthworms, play an important role. Animals are used in rampant vegetation control, fire control, biogas generation, pollination, soil aeration, humus and soil production, seed distribution, pest control and as a source of food, manure, heat and power.

Keeping any animals in a permaculture system requires good management. Earthworms need a constant supply of food, oxygen, water and shelter from sunlight. The acidity of the bedding material is important too. Earthworms do not like food materials which are too acidic or too alkaline – such as onions and lemons.

Hothouses

Seedlings and frost-susceptible plants should be maintained during the colder winter months in a hothouse. A hothouse, which is also known as a greenhouse, is a structure where energy is stored as heat, and this heat can then radiate into the surrounding air. Hothouses can extend the growing season of some vegetable crops, such as melons, and they allow other vegetables, such as tomatoes, to be grown all year round. The orientation of the hothouse is important. It should have a long axis running east-west, with one long side facing south, as you want it to receive as much sunlight as possible during the winter. Windows should be installed for ventilation and to help in the regulation of the temperature inside the hothouse. Ideally, a hothouse should be attached to the house – along some part of the southern side where warm air in winter can be ducted or drawn into the house.

Mini-hothouse

The first project is to make a simple cover for germinating seeds in propagation trays. A similar project, called a mini greenhouse, was described in the Recycling Plastic Bottles activity.

What you need

✤ Metal hanging basket frames.

✤ Clear or translucent plastic sheeting – even shopping bags are suitable.

✤ Germination or seedling trays. You can purchase these from most nurseries. Alternatively, recycle margarine containers as the trays.

✤ Potting mix for seedlings.

What you do

✤ Place your seeds or young seedlings in a tray. These seedling trays normally measure about 25 x 30cm.

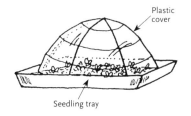

Plastic cover

Seedling tray

Figure 52. Using a hanging basket for a mini-greenhouse.

❋ Cut some plastic sheeting, or a recycled plastic shopping bag, so that it fits over an inverted hanging basket.

❋ Place the hanging basket over the tray and position it in the warmth of the winter sunlight.

❋ Check the tray periodically, every day or two, to make sure that the seeds have germinated and that the seedlings are not drying out.

Cold Frame

A cold frame is a simple box with a glass lid so that heat is trapped and everything inside is kept warm. This is an ideal structure to germinate and maintain seedlings until they are ready to be planted out and the danger of frosts is over. Place the cold frame directly in the winter sunlight.

What you need

❋ Recycled window frames – at least one, but 2 or 3 would be optimum.

❋ Timber planks, such as second-hand, 10cm floorboards.

❋ 50 x 25mm roofing battens.

❋ Hinges – 1 pair per window.

❋ Handles or knobs.

❋ Screws or bolts for hinges.

❋ 100g of 25mm nails.

Figure 53. A typical cold frame.

What you do

❉ Cut the timber planks or floorboards to make a box the same size as your window frame. Most wooden window frames are about 1 to 1.2m long and half as wide.

❉ The box should be three floorboards high (30cm), with the final board being cut at an angle so that the window lid rests at this angle towards the sun. This means the sides will taper from the top of the third floorboard at the back to the top of the second board at the front (*see figure 53*). If you use narrower floorboards, such as 75mm width, make the box four boards high.

❉ Use the roofing batten timber to strengthen the corners – one piece for each of the four corners of the box. Nail or screw the boards to the batten or to each other.

❉ A floor is not necessary as you can place the cold frame directly onto the ground or onto concrete or even a bench top. However, floorboards can also be used for a base and these should be nailed or screwed into place.

❉ The window lid needs to be hinged with at least two hinges attached to the back of the box. Screw or bolt the hinges in place.

Larger Hothouse

If you are serious about propagation and producing certain vegetables in winter then you need a more sophisticated hothouse. The one described below can be made relatively inexpensively if you buy new materials or cheaper still if you obtain second-hand or recycled materials.

What you need

❉ 3 sheets of 6 x 2.4m concrete slab mesh (6mm iron rod).

❉ Old full-length fly-wire door and wooden frame.

* PVC tape or heavy duty masking tape.

* 12 x 6m clear plastic sheeting to cover hothouse. Buy UV-stabilised plastic if this is possible.

* Tie wire or welder.

* Old pipe or garden stakes.

* Second-hand sleepers or bricks.

* Clouts.

* Small, second-hand timber-framed window, which can be opened.

* Bolt cutters or hacksaw.

* PVC pipe and mini sprinklers for reticulation.

What you do

* Lay two sheets of mesh side by side on the ground.

* Weld or tie securely together with wire.

* Arch the sheets to form a semi-circle with a width of about 4m. It should be high enough to stand in. You will need to get someone to give you a hand to hold this structure in place.

* Support the position of the structure so that it doesn't move. This can be accomplished by driving pipe or garden stakes, in three equidistant positions against the frame, into the ground. Alternatively, weld a piece of 6mm rod from one side to the other, or use fencing wire to do the same thing.

* Cut the other weld mesh sheet in half – one half for each end.

* Stand the mesh against each end and, using the bolt cutters or hacksaw, trim the excess mesh so that a neat fit is obtained.

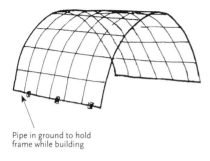

Pipe in ground to hold
frame while building

Figure 54. Building a mesh hothouse.

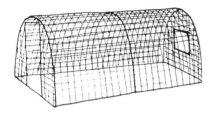

Figure 55. The final structure.
A window should be placed
opposite a door for cross
ventilation.

Weld or tie the end mesh to the main structure.

❀ One end needs a door and the other end needs a window (for ventilation). Cut the mesh to fit the door or window frame. Use wooden door and window frames because you can secure the mesh to the frame easily by using fencing nails (horseshoe shaped).

❀ Replace the flywire or panels on the door with clear plastic. Use UV-stabilised plastic if you want the hothouse to last a few years.

❀ Drape plastic sheeting over the main frame and bury the ends under the ground or place sleepers or bricks on top to hold it in place.

❀ If you have jagged or rough edges on the mesh use masking tape to cover them before you place the plastic on top.

❀ Cut the plastic for each end, allowing extra for the overlap with the rest of the structure, and then cut out where the window or door frames are. Nail the plastic to the wooden frames.

❀ Overlap the plastic from each end across the main frame and tape down with broad masking tape. A commercial product called Ziplock is used by nurseries to join the main plastic sheeting to the ends. Ziplock is a length of aluminium track which holds the plastic sheeting in place by the use of a hard plastic strip. When you buy the plastic sheeting ask how the ends can be joined. There may be similar products in other parts of the world.

✤ Plants need water and it is important that you provide a water source in the hothouse. The simplest system is to have some PVC pipe suspended along the side walls and connect this to a tap. Small spray nozzles (misters) are placed along the pipe – say 1m apart. A five to ten minute spray at least once each day will be sufficient to keep the humidity up and the plants alive. Water more frequently if you have lots of seedlings coming on.

From A Permaculture Perspective

A simple example of a passive solar system is the hothouse or greenhouse. In a passive system heat flow is not controlled or directed. The sun heats the air inside the greenhouse to provide warm growing conditions for plants. The most efficient greenhouses are made from glass. Solar radiation easily passes through glass and is absorbed by the plants, pots, benches, floor and other objects inside the greenhouse. These objects re-radiate some of this absorbed energy as heat. Heat does not travel through glass very well and it is trapped inside the greenhouse. In summer, the heat inside the greenhouse would be far too hot for plants, which are normally now kept in a shadehouse. Hothouses are most useful during the colder, winter months. This is a direct gain system as solar radiation can directly enter into the hothouse. If you live in particularly cold areas you could provide some extra form of heat storage for your hothouse. Two of the simplest ways are to use water or rock.

You can fill 200l drums with water and use these as supports for a work-bench. Alternatively pile some rocks along the length of the northern side of the hothouse. These will absorb heat during the day and slowly radiate it out during the night. Insulate the southern wall and the southern part of the east and west walls with polystyrene foam sheeting.

In a home, passive solar design decreases energy costs and increases comfort levels for the occupants. The following house and garden design features are relevant for both hemispheres.

Some passive design features in a home would include:

✲ Long axis in east-west direction.

✲ Insulation in the ceilings and walls, especially the north, east and west walls.

✲ Roof eaves large enough on the southern side to shade all of the wall in the summer. Usually this will mean an eave of 75cm or less.

✲ Minimum windows on the east and west sides.

✲ Correct positioning of windows and air vents to allow cross-flow ventilation by winds.

✲ Appropriate building materials which have a high thermal mass to store heat during winter. Materials would include conventional bricks, mudbricks, rammed earth, stone and concrete.

✲ Correct pitch of the roof for solar hot water system panels and for venting of hot air from the house in summer.

Besides house design, landscape features around the house can greatly affect energy use. Trees and shrubs can be used to reduce heating and cooling costs. In particular:

✲ Plant windbreaks to reduce heat loss during the winter months.

✲ Avoid concrete and paving along the southern side of the house, which will reflect light into the house and heat it up during summer.

However, this feature would be good in winter if deciduous trees were planted along the northern side of the path.

The path would be shaded in summer, but able to absorb heat during winter when the trees are bare and have lost their leaves.

✲ Plant deciduous trees, creepers, vines and shrubs along the southern side of the house and also about half-way down the eastern and western sides. This will provide added protection from the summer sun, and it is especially important to shade the western side of the house.

Shadehouses

Shade protection of plants is important during the summer. Shade prevents excessive water loss, leaf burn and damage to flowers, and protects young seedlings from desiccation. Shade also reduces the amount of water each plant needs. Shadehouses can be attached to the northern side of a house. Cool air from the shadehouse can be drawn into the house during hot days.

A Simple Shadehouse

This is a free-standing shadehouse. However, it can be attached to a house, using at least one wall as part of the structure. The best location is on the northern wall and if a window opens into the shadehouse the cold air can be directed through the house to cool it.

What you need

* 5 poles x 2.lm long.

* 15 lengths of roofing batten, 75 x 30mm.

* 75mm nails.

* One pair of hinges.

* 50 - 80% shade cloth.

* Old fly wire door.

* One packet (500g) 25mm clouts.

* Optional – 2 dozen triple grips.

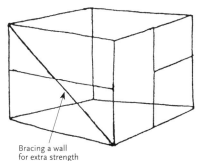

Bracing a wall for extra strength

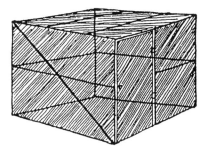

Figure 56. Building the frame for the shadehouse, leading to the finished product.

What you do

Make a square or rectangular frame, using four of the poles as verticals, big enough for your needs or using the space you have available. A useful size would be 3.5 x 2.5m.

✿ The fifth pole is used to make the door frame. Each pole can be buried 20cm to prevent movement.

✿ Nail the roofing battens to join each pole and across from one side to the other for the roof.

✿ You should have battens at the top, bottom and middle of each side – and preferably more if you have plenty of timber. For extra rigidity, you can secure a batten at an angle between the poles to form a brace.

✿ The roof needs extra battens, even though shade cloth is quite light. Battens can be further secured by nailing a triple grip between the batten and pole, using 25mm clouts.

✿ Hang the door by a couple of hinges.

✿ Drape the shadecloth over the structure, cut away the door and nail the shade cloth to the frame, using clouts. You should at least cover the roof and halfway down each side. Full coverage by shade cloth is obviously the best.

A Geodesic Dome

A geodesic dome is a special structure which is very strong and very easy to make. It only has two different lengths of pipe. These lengths are multiples of 273 and 309. In a 6m length of PVC pipe you can get 3 side lengths each of 1,950mm (cut off the bell housing at the end of the pipe). This side is 6.3 x 309 = 1,950mm. You can multiply the 309 number by anything else to get any length of side you want. We used 6.3 because it will give you the greatest length of sides from a standard 6m length of PVC water pipe. If you multiply 6.3 x 273 you get 1,720mm, the length of the other size. The structure of the dome is a series of pentagons and hexagons with small triangles within these. The triangle is one of the strongest structures known.

What you need

✿ 22 lengths of 25mm Class 9 PVC water irrigation pipe – each length is normally 6m.

✿ Shadecloth – 10 x 10m (you will have to sow strips of shadecloth together).

✿ 26 of 50mm bolts, 6mm diameter, with washers.

✿ Hacksaw.

✿ 6mm drill bit and drill.

✿ Source of heat, such as a gas cooker or barbecue.

✿ Wooden press.

✿ Wooden templates – one at 1,720mm long and another at 1,950mm long.

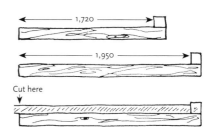

Figure 57. The templates for the dome sides.

What you do

✿ Cut 10 lengths of 6m PVC pipe into segments 1,720mm long (3 each in every 6m pipe). Don't start at the bell housing end. You need 30 short pipe lengths.

✿ Cut 12 lengths of 6m PVC pipe using the 1,950mm template.

✿ You need 35 of these longer lengths. There will be 1 spare length.

✿ Heat or soften each end of the pipe by rolling it above a heat source for about 30 seconds.

64

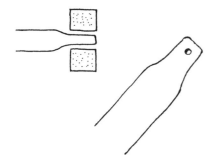

Figure 58. Flattening the pipe.

✽ Quickly flatten the ends by placing them between 2 pieces of timber, which act as a press. Hold the PVC pipe still for 1 minute until the plastic has hardened again.

✽ Drill a 6mm hole about 25mm from each end of each pipe.

✽ Now comes the assembly which is initially done by laying the pipe out on the ground. Make a pentagon using 5 short lengths for the internal part and 5 long lengths for the external shape. Bolt the 5 short lengths together in the middle.

✽ To each corner of the pentagon add 2 long and 1 short length of pipe. Bolt each corner – there will be 4 long and 2 short to bolt together.

✽ To each end of the short lengths add 2 more short pipes. Do not bolt yet.

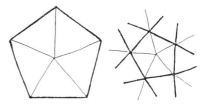

Figure 59. Starting the dome.

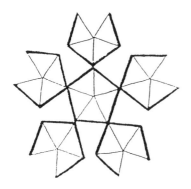

Figure 60. Joining the pipes together.

✽ Where there are 3 ends add 2 short lengths and bolt all 5 together to make another centre of a pentagon.

✽ Where there are 4 ends (2 long and 2 short) add another 2 long lengths. The dome will have to be raised to be able to bolt all of these together. You will either need some helpers or you can lift the structure up and rest it on a sturdy ladder or 200l drum.

❉ Add the 10 remaining long lengths of pipe around the base.

❉ You should end up with a structure that has a pentagon for a roof, and from each corner of this pentagon there will be another pentagon shape. From each side of the initial pentagon you should be able to recognise a hexagon.

❉ Drape the shadecloth over the structure and tuck underneath the pipe at the base. Cut a doorway at some appropriate position, so that the shadecoth can be pushed back when you want to enter.

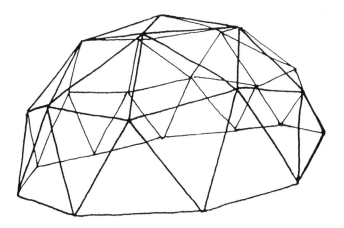

Figure 61. The finished geodesic dome.

From a Permaculture Perspective

Structures such as shadehouses and hothouses are positioned in particular zones around the house. A zone is a region within the property, starting from Zone 0 (the building), Zone 1, Zone 2 and up to Zone 5. Plants, animals, objects and structures are placed in a particular zone depending on the number of times you have to visit them. Vegetables and herbs, which you pick every day, are placed closest to the house, in Zone 1.

Zone 1, which generally surrounds the house, usually only contains plants in intensively cultivated garden beds. Animals are usually introduced in Zone 2. The chicken or duck pen and earthworm farm, as well as the tool shed, shadehouse and hothouse (if these are not attached to the house) are often found in this area. There will also be more garden beds and maybe some fruit trees, but these gardens and trees need less visiting than those from which you harvest every day.

Zone 3 is mainly for small acreage properties. It might contain an orchard, geese, bee hives and/or a milking goat.

Zone 4 is for broad acre farms and this area might contain dams, agroforestry, shelterbelts, stock fodder lock-up areas, crops and windmills.

Zone 5 is natural bush or wilderness, which helps to support the native animals in an area.

Urban properties might only contain Zones land 2 (and hopefully a small area set aside for natural local species planted or replanted in Zone 5).

Small acreage properties (less than 5 ha) have Zones 1, 2, 3 and 5 while larger properties have all five Zones.

Animal Tractors

Animal tractors are portable pens. They are most useful for small animals such as poultry, guinea pigs, rabbits and quail. Small pigs and lambs can also be kept in larger varieties of these simple structures.

The uses of animal tractors are many. They include preparing (by tilling and fertilising) the ground for vegetable growing, removing rampant weed species such as oxalis, kikuyu and onion weed, removing plants for fire control and utilising minimum space while still providing a continuous source of food for the animals. In some situations, the width of the 'tractor' becomes the width of the garden bed – the weeds are removed and the ground fertilised, ready for planting.

The 'tractors' can be large or small, more-or-less fixed or totally portable, dragged around or moved on wheels, and made from a variety of materials. For example, you can use timber but it can be very awkward and heavy. Conduit or tubular steel (curtain rod size) is quite light for the strength it possesses. The structure needs to be light so that one person can easily move it. Adding the netting and sheet metal further increases the stability and strength.

What you need

�֍ 6 x 2m lengths of metal conduit (curtain rod), solid rod (8 mm diameter) or square tube.

✤ 6mm diameter bolts, 30mm long, with nuts.

✤ Chicken wire (bird netting size mesh), 2m wide and 4m long.

✤ Flat sheet metal 3.6m x 60cm.

✤ Old wooden broom handle or pole.

✤ Drill, with 6 and 3mm bits.

✤ Hammer.

* Hacksaw.

* 4 x 25mm screws or clouts.

* Tie wire.

* One pair of hinges.

* Latch for door.

* Pop rivets and gun.

* Optional: welder, wheels – such as on a lawnmower.

What you do

* Use the hacksaw to cut 3 lengths of 2m conduit or square tube in half. These segments will form the sides of the triangular pen. If using solid 8mm rod you should use a welder to join the rod together.

* Use a hammer to flatten about 30mm of the conduit or tube at each end of these shorter pieces so they can be joined together easily.

* Drill a 6mm hole at each end.

* Repeat for the 3 longer pieces of conduit or tube, but flatten about 65 - 70mm so that each end can be folded over at right angles and drilled at the end.

* The shorter pieces make a triangle for the ends of the pen while the longer pieces are used to provide the length for the pen and to join the ends.

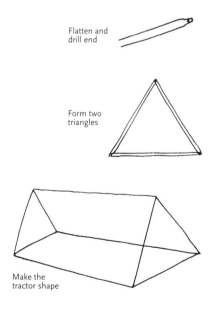

Flatten and drill end

Form two triangles

Make the tractor shape

Figure 62. Starting the animal tractor.

69

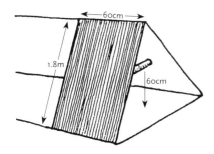

Figure 63. Adding the end cover and roost.

* Bolt the conduit pieces together.

* Fold the chicken wire over the main frame and tie to the conduit or tube. Place and tie chicken wire on only one end. Chicken wire should go on the bottom if foxes are a danger, you want to keep rabbits or guinea pigs in the pen or you don't want little chickens to escape.

* One end will include the roost and door. Fold or cut the sheet metal to make a cover on the top two sides at this end. Drill 3mm holes and rivet the sheet metal to the frame. The base does not have sheet metal.

* The roost is made by cutting a broom handle to length so that it can be secured from one side of the sheet metal to the other. Use the drill and 3mm bit to make holes through the sheet metal and into the timber end of the pole. Secure with at least two screws at each end. The pole should be positioned horizontally and located about 60cm from the ground.

* The door is made by putting the sheet metal in two sections at this same end. Since the sheet metal is 60cm wide, this will be the width of the door. Cut another piece of metal for the top part and secure this with pop rivets.

* Hinge the bottom door by riveting the hinge to the sheet metal and to the frame.

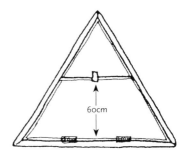

Figure 64. Making the door.

* Rivet a latch to the door and top part of the end. The door should open outwards.

70

* Optional: mount a pair of wheels onto one end so that you can move the tractor around more easily. You will need to fix a couple of axles to the frame – either by welding or bolting them on. A handle fitted to the top of the tractor will enable it to be moved easily.

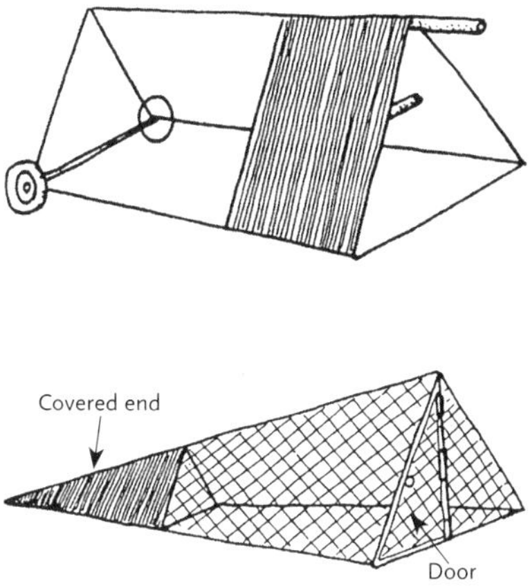

Figure 65. *Top*: Adding wheels makes the tractor easy to move. *Bottom*: Another type of animal

Another 'tractor' can be made from concrete floor mesh. Use a piece 2.4m long and 1.8m wide. Bend the mesh to form an elliptical shape (like an egg shape) about 1m wide and 80cm high.

Use some mesh to make each end. You can either weld or tie these on with wire depending on your resources. Cover with chicken wire and provide a door and perch as before.

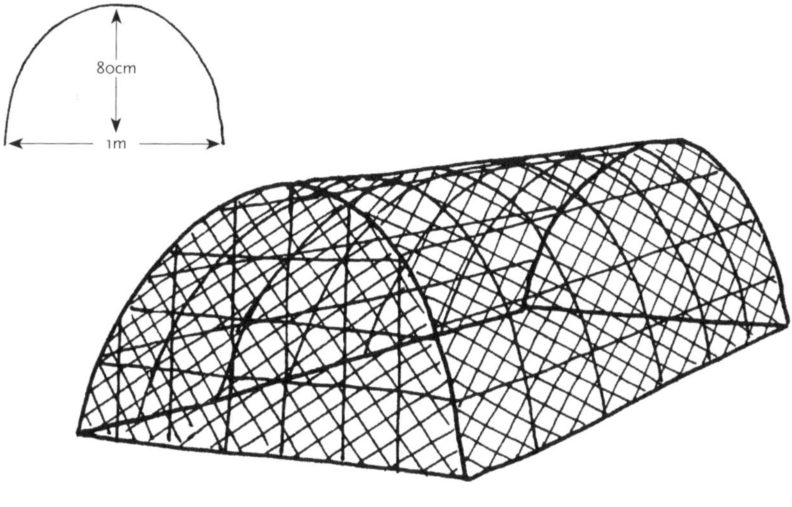

Figure 66. An animal tractor made from concrete mesh is simple to construct.

From A Permaculture Perspective

Animal tractors and garden beds are positioned in particular zones as discussed in the activity shadehouses. Another consideration in placement of structures and objects in a permaculture design is that of 'sector planning'. Sector planning considers the energies that move through a system. These energies include wind, sunlight and fire.

Other things which are included in the sector analysis include rain, flooding and aesthetic views.

You might want some deciduous fruit trees in Zone 2, so you would also put them in an area where there is a potential fire danger as these types of trees are fire tolerant and will tend to slow down a fire should it pass through. Or you could put them in a chicken run so that the chickens will clean up rotten fruit and help control pests, including fruit fly.

Some of the things you would put in a design as part of sector planning include windbreak trees and shrubs, deciduous trees along the southern, western and eastern sides of your house, fire retardant plant species in areas where fire could enter the property, dams and ponds in fire danger areas, shelterbelts for larger properties, and trees which are high water users in areas that flood.

You could even put your shadehouse, hothouse or tool shed in a sector to further act as a windbreak.

Animal tractors can be placed in areas where there are grasses, weeds or pioneer species so that these can be maintained or eliminated. This is another example of sector planning for fire control in this area.

Environmentally Responsible Living

Much of the pollution that humans experience comes from the home. Have you ever considered how much air pollution we cause when we indiscriminately use chemically-based hair sprays, non-biodegradable cleaning agents, toxic dry-cleaning fluids and preservatives in carpets and upholstery? And what's more – we're breathing all of this in every day! There are many things that you can do about protecting our environment and making it a better, safer place to bring up your children and grandchildren. Some of these include recycling used lard and oil to make natural soap, reconstituting paper so that it can be re-used and making safe household cleaning products. The following activities will show you how to be more environmentally responsible and how to do your bit to conserve our limited resources.

Making Soap

The production of soap is one way that used kitchen fat and oil can be recycled. Sodium hydroxide is a poisonous substance and should be handled with extreme caution. Use safety glasses and rubber gloves whenever you use caustic soda. It will burn the skin and it should not be heated directly. The following recipe will make about 2kg of soap.

What you need

❀ 200g sodium hydroxide (caustic soda).

❀ 1kg lard (pigfat) or 1l cooking oil (such as olive and sunflower oils).

❀ Large iron or stainless steel saucepan.

❀ 500ml water, milk or herb tea (such as rose petal or chamomile).

❀ Iced water.

* 200ml methylated spirits.

* Cotton cloth, to filter soap flakes.

* Fermentation bin.

* Small dishes or containers for your 'cakes' of soap.

* Optional: perfume, honey, rolled oats or food colouring.

What you do

* Melt the lard or heat the oil in an iron or stainless steel saucepan. Don't use an aluminium pan as sodium hydroxide will react with it.

* Dissolve the sodium hydroxide in a large plastic bowl which contains the water, milk or herb tea solution. Sodium hydroxide will etch glass and ceramic bowls. Slowly add the caustic soda pellets to the water and stir to dissolve them. The solution will become very hot.

* Pour 200ml of methylated spirits into the sodium hydroxide solution.

* Carefully pour this solution into the melted lard. Optional: at this stage you can add 100ml honey.

* Heat for a further 15-20 minutes. A solid should start to form.

* Remove from the stove and allow to cool. (If no soap flakes have formed, add 100ml of a strong solution of salt water.)

* Filter the soap from the solution by passing it through a cloth suspended over a fermentation bin.

* Wash the flakes several times with iced water. This removes excess caustic soda.

* Optional: add a few drops of perfume or food colouring to the soap. Rolled oats and honey are excellent additives to make a natural, cleansing soap. Mix all or any of these in the flakes.

✤ Place the flakes into dishes or small containers and allow to set. This may take a few days or a week or more.

✤ Test some of your soap flakes by adding some to a jar of water. Shake vigorously – the soap will lather.

Hand-made Paper

Paper is made from the pulp of trees. Several thousand trees are cut down each week to produce the weekend papers in capital cities. Demand for trees has outstripped their growth and replacement. Recycling paper has become law in some countries, such as Germany, and it won't be long before paper will have to be recycled in every country. Newspaper can be used for this activity, but if it contains too much ink the paper which is made will be grey. White photocopying and computer paper are the best.

What you need

✤ Deckle. This is a wooden frame which has a tightly stretched screen secured to it. Make a deckle about 30cm square with fly-wire or shadecloth as the screen. Screw or nail the timber frame together and then stretch and glue the screen over the frame.

Figure 67. Making a deckle.

✤ Waste paper. Clean white paper is best – avoid colourful, glossy magazines.

✤ Electric blender or food processor.

✤ Large tank or baby's bath.

✤ Felt or cloth, large enough to cover deckle.

✤ Optional: electric iron, flat plywood sheet, food colouring, bricks or weights.

What you do

✤ Tear the paper into small pieces and place them into a food blender.

✤ Fill with water and blend for a minute or two – long enough to completely mash the paper and make a mixture with a thin consistency.

✤ Pour the mixture into a large trough or tank.

✤ Repeat two or three times to partly fill the bottom of the trough.

✤ Add an equal volume of water to your paper mixture.

✤ Slide the deckle underneath the mixture and carefully raise it out. You might have to hand mix the paper mixture when the deckle is in the trough.

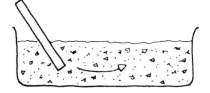

✤ As you lift the deckle out of the trough give it a gentle tap to drain the excess water and help spread the paper fibres.

Figure 68. Slide the deckle underneath the water surface.

✤ Turn the deckle over and place it on a piece of felt or cloth, even an old handkerchief. Some coloured felts may 'run'.

✤ Rub the screen so that the paper fibres will become separated from the deckle. Excess water can be wiped away with another cloth.

✤ Carefully pull the deckle frame off the felt. The paper should remain behind.

✤ Cover the paper sheet with another piece of felt or cloth to help it dry faster.

✤ Before the paper dries completely, gently pull the paper sheet off the felt.

✽ Optional: use an electric iron to heat and dry the paper sheet. Don't have the iron too hot as you will burn the paper. The newly made paper sheets can also be placed between plywood panels to flatten them. Add weights or bricks to help squeeze excess water out. To make coloured paper, which is a little patchy, add a few drops of food colouring to the paper solution before you lift the deckle out.

Household Cleaning Products

Great news! You can clean almost all of your house, including some of those stubborn stains, with the use of a few natural substances that are cheap to buy and easy to obtain.

This activity is not set out as we have done previously. There are no 'steps' to make cleaning agents – each of the following substances are most often used by themselves. You will find a short description of each substance and what they can be used for in your home.

What you need

✽ **Vinegar (white).**
Vinegar is a dilute solution of acetic acid. Vinegar is used as a bleach, disinfectant, deodorant, and anti-mould cleaner.

✽ **Bicarbonate of soda, baking soda (sodium hydrogen carbonate).**
Bicarbonate of soda is an excellent general purpose cleaner which can be used as a powder or as a solution.

✽ **Borax (sodium borate).**
Borax is poisonous so handle it with care. It is used as a fabric and water softener, stain remover, bleach and disinfectant.

✽ **Tea tree or eucalyptus oil.**
Tea tree oil comes from the leaves of *Melaleuca alternifolia*, a native plant to eastern Australia. It is one of nature's most remarkable antiseptics and disinfectants. Eucalyptus oil comes from the leaves of eucalyptus trees. Like tea tree oil, it is a strong antiseptic which

will kill many organisms. The oil of gum leaves is also used in the treatment of colds and influenza and as an additive to your clothes washing to remove greasy or oily stains.

✤ **Cloudy ammonia (ammonium hydroxide solution).**
Although cloudy ammonia can irritate the eyes and smells obnoxious, it quickly breaks down in the environment. It is a powerful bleach and cleaning agent.

✤ **Lemon juice (fresh).**
Lemon juice is a weak solution of citric acid and is a mild bleach, deodorant and cleaning agent.

✤ **Pure soap.**
Pure soap is a sodium salt of an organic acid (a carboxylate). Soap is a surfactant or wetting agent which allows water to combine with greasy substances so that they can be removed from dishes and clothing. Use the soap which you have made in one of the previous activities. Pure soap is totally biodegradable. Commercial brands include Velvet and Preservene.

✤ **Steel wool.**
Very effective abrasive for stubborn dirt and stains.

THE KITCHEN

To clean:

✤ Dishes: Grated soap flakes, vigorously stirred to form a lather. You can buy old-fashioned soap shakers at some hardware and camping stores.

✤ Ovens, hotplates: Use cloudy ammonia, or scrub with damp bicarb soda (used in this book to mean bicarbonate of soda).

Figure 69. A soap shaker is used to generate soap suds to clean dishes.

❀ Burnt saucepans: Cover the base with vinegar or damp bicarb soda and leave overnight. Use steel wool and a little water the next day. For stubborn marks boil some vinegar in the pan for five minutes.

❀ Benchtops and sinks: Sponge with damp bicarb soda or borax.

❀ Tiles: Wipe with vinegar on a sponge.

THE LAUNDRY

To clean:

❀ Floors: Use cloudy ammonia or vinegar.

❀ Washing machine or troughs. Sponge with damp bicarbonate of soda or borax.

❀ Clothes: Grated soap flakc made into a solution. Add quarter of a cup of borax and 5ml of eucalyptus oil for greasy clothes. To whiten clothes add a small amount of borax, lemon juice or cloudy ammoma.

❀ Tiles: Wipe with vinegar and steel wool or bicarb soda on a sponge.

❀ Stains on clothes. Wipe a small amount of tea tree oil or eucalyptus oil on the stain before washing. Some stains can be removed by using borax, vinegar, lemon juice or cloudy ammonia.

THE BATHROOM

To clean:

❀ Mirrors: Cloudy ammonia, vinegar or borax solution.

❀ Plastic shower curtains: Scrub with vinegar and hang in the sun.

❀ Baths and basins: Steel wool with damp bicarb soda or borax.

❋ Moulds on tiles: Vinegar, cloudy ammonia or bicarb soda.

❋ Toilet bowl and cistern: Wipe with vinegar or leave half a cup of vinegar in the bowl overnight.

Figure 70. Use vinegar and steel wool to remove mould and stains from kitchen and bathroom wall and tiles.

PERSONAL HYGIENE AND TOILETRIES

For a:

✤ Deodorant: Use bicarb soda, either in powder form or as a spray-on solution.

✤ Hair rinse: Use diluted vinegar or lemon juice.

✤ Toothpaste: Use bicarb soda, mixed with a little salt.

✤ Shine to jewellery: Soak gold in cloudy ammonia for ten minutes, dip copper in weak vinegar or rub with a paste of bicarb soda and lemon juice, and clean silver by dipping it in a hot solution of bicarb soda which contains a small piece of aluminium foil. Aluminium and stainless steel are simply cleaned by using warm soapy water and a little bicarb soda.

✤ Shampoo: Use bicarb soda for a dry shampoo and brush out or lemon juice and a beaten egg and then rinse.

From A Permaculture Perspective

One of the most important aspects of permaculture is its ethics. These were briefly discussed in the section on *What is Permaculture* at the beginning of this book.

One of these ethics was 'Care of the Earth'. Many of the sprays, deodorants, laundry cleaning agents and body care products that you may have used in the past and that many others are still using, are slowly poisoning our own families and the environment.

There is an extremely fine line between human desires and ecological disaster. We are slowly destroying the balance that exists between the organisms which live in our environment. Our production of expensive, chemically-based cleaners, insecticides and herbicides intensifies these problems.

It is only when humans reflect on the use of such substances, or investigate and realise the long term effects of their actions, that we moderate or abandon the kinds of things which ultimately threaten our own survival.

Earthcare is the first permaculture ethic, which itself is all encompassing, as all other ethics arise from and are included in it. We have a responsibility to care for all living and non-living things. This includes all plants and animals, the soil and the environment. The earthcare ethic implies the ethical use of resources, active conservation and the rehabilitation of our fragile Earth. Humans need to plan for sustainability and to moderate their actions.

In permaculture systems we should be minimising our impact on the environment by using renewable energy sources such as wind, solar and water energies, using native species wherever possible in the system, cultivating the least amount of land by growing food in intensive systems, developing community responsibility and then assisting others to become self-reliant.

Hay Box Cooker

The hay box cooker is a simple technology which enables you to cook food using less energy. Originally this type of cooker was made by insulating a wooden box with dry hay or straw. Nowadays, we have a greater range of other insulating materials, such as polystyrene balls (in bean bags). You don't even have to use a wooden box – cardboard works well, so does an old refrigerator or freezer on its side, and it is possible to just use a bean bag. This activity shows you how to make a more sophisticated bag which will cook your evening meals slowly and efficiently. The hay box cooker works well for rice, stews and soups. It can also be used to keep food warm for long periods of time. You bring the pot to the boil as you would do normally on a conventional stove and then you place it in the hay box cooker. Make sure that the lid is on tight as you do not want any heat to be lost from the insulated box.

What you need

❊ Bag of polystyrene balls (from an old bean bag). Other insulating materials you can use include wool, vermiculite, straw or shredded newspaper. Even solid slabs of unshredded newspaper will work.

❊ Cotton cloth, about 3 x lm (3m^2).

❊ Needle and thread.

❊ Butcher's paper.

❊ Pencil, pen or texta.

❊ Ruler and tape measure.

❊ Scissors.

What you do

❊ The first step is to make the pattern for the base and lid. Using the instructions that follow, mark out a pattern on butcher's paper or something similar. You will need a sheet of paper – about 1m^2 – to make both patterns.

❉ To make the base pattern: measure a line 80cm long on the paper.

❉ From one end mark a point 24cm in, and from the other end a point 16cm (*see fig 71*).

Figure 71

❉ Draw perpendicular lines through these points which will be 24cm or l6cm respectively.

❉ Draw parallel lines at these new positions. These will be parallel to the original main line (*see fig 72*).

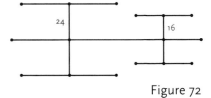

Figure 72

❉ Mark off a position 20cm from the 24cm end and 12cm from the 16cm end on these new lines.

❉ Join the two sets of lines as shown on the right (*see fig 73*).

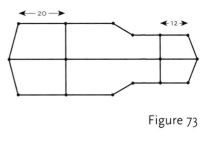

Figure 73

❉ To make the lid: draw a main line 64cm long. Bisect this line to find the middle at 32cm (*see fig 74*). Draw a line perpendicular either side of the mainline.

❉ Mark off points which are 24cm from the main line. Draw parallel lines (to the main line) at these new points (*see fig 75*).

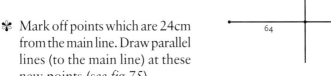

Figure 74

84

✤ Come along 12cm either side of the perpendicular lines and mark these points. Draw a line from these points to the ends of the main line (*see fig 76*).

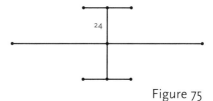

Figure 75

✤ You have now drawn the basic pattern for the lid segments.

✤ Use this pattern and the other larger one (for the base) to mark the cloth. Cut out four of each shape from the cotton cloth.

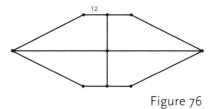

Figure 76

✤ Sew the four shapes of any one type together to make a football. Allow 5mm hems when sewing. Leave one edge unsewn so that you can fill the bag with polystyrene balls.

✤ Loosely fill the bags with the polystyrene or shredded newspaper (about two-thirds full) and sew the final edge.

✤ Insert the larger base bag into a cardboard box. The smaller lid has to fit in snugly to retain heat.

✤ Boil your food and place it within the cooker. The lid is positioned and the cooker left for a few hours. This is a trial and error cooking method. The more you practise, the more you'll know how long to leave it in the cooker. For example, rice only needs about half an hour in the haybox cooker, while stews take at least twice this long.

Figure 77. Cross section of the hay box cooker.

85

From A Permaculture Perspective

One of the main principles of permaculture is efficient energy planning. This is accomplished when we place all of the elements in our design in particular zones and sectors (which manage incoming energy to the system). Zones and sectors have already been discussed in other activities.

Efficient energy planning equates to efficient economic planning, as Bill Mollison points out in his text *Introduction to Permaculture* (1994).

We make every effort to put in structures that will produce or conserve energy, rather than structures which will continuously consume energy.

Our aim is to catch, store, cycle and use energy before it is lost from the system.

In the same way, we encourage people to grow their own food in their own backyard or community plot, rather than transporting and buying it in from distant farms and cities. What's more, locally produced organic produce will be fresh and healthy.

Transport costs add enormous costs to food. Transport vehicles also consume precious fossil fuels and contribute to atmospheric pollution. Water harvesting is another consideration in design work. We construct dams and ponds uphill so that water can be directed down the slopes, by using gravity, to garden areas.

This system of water management can also permit us to generate energy by using technology such as pelton wheels and micro-hydro plants.

If we make our own electricity on site we further conserve global energy resources.

Determining Levels

A variety of methods are used to measure slopes and levels. If you do not have access to an optical instrument, such as a dumpy level or a theodolite, you can make do with an A frame level or a water level (colloquially called a bunyip level). Both of these are easy to make and the materials you require are inexpensive.

'A' Frame Level

This is a useful device which marks out contours for building retaining walls and garden beds, and determines levels of building slabs and driveways.

'A' frame levels are mainly useful for small areas, such as backyards. They are not useful over long distances, especially if accuracy is required. While an 'A' frame level is easy to move around bushes and trees, it is often too slow on larger areas in the paddock.

What you need

❀ 3 pieces of timber: 2 x 2.5m lengths and l x l.5m length of 50 x 25mm (2 x 1in). Roofing batten is ideal but bamboo, pine and even reasonable branches can be used.

❀ 3 bolts to secure timber.

❀ Builder's spirit level, 1.2m (4ft) or any other bubble level.

❀ Masking tape or fixing straps or string.

❀ Optional: Tin lids and nails (clouts).

What you do

❀ Cut the longer poles to the same length.

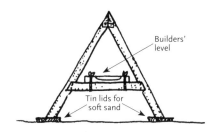

Figure 78. An 'A' frame level.

❧ Measure down 1m from each end and drill holes so that the shorter cross piece can be secured and the longer poles can pivot on one end.

❧ Secure the level with strong tape, string or straps.

❧ Optional: If you frequently work in sandy areas, one variation of this basic structure is to nail tin lids (e.g. Milo tins) to the bottom of the legs. The wooden legs tend to sink when you swivel them so lids reduce this problem.

❧ When using the level to mark out a contour or gentle slope, swivel one leg to a new position so that the bubble is in the middle of the level. This means that the vertical position of each leg is the same, i.e. they are level.

Bunyip (Water) Level

The Egyptians used the principle that water seeks its own level to build the Pyramids. The accuracy inlaying the large stone blocks and the levelness of the walls is unsurpassed today. We can use water to find or confirm the horizontal level of buildings, contours on a slope, swales and irrigation drains.

What you need

❧ 2 x lm clear plastic tubing.

❧ Garden hose or 13mm black polypipe.

❧ 2 x l3mm poly or copper pipe joiners.

❧ 2 small corks or rubber stoppers to fit tubing.

❧ 2 x 1m rulers (or sticks or poles the same length). It is easier to

88

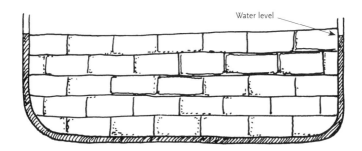

Figure 79. The difference in water height indicates that the brick course is too high on one side. This can be corrected over the next few courses by using less mortar between the brick layers on this side.

just buy the full length of clear plastic tubing, but this is often more expensive than a smaller piece fixed at each end of a common garden hose or poly (irrigation) pipe.

What you do

❊ Use a pipe joiner to attach one piece of clear plastic tubing to either end of a garden hose or black polypipe.

❊ The hose is filled with water, making sure that air bubbles are allowed to escape while filling. You will know if this is done properly because the water should be at the same level when the two ends are held together. If the level is different in the hose ends, an air bubble may be present in the hose. Gently tap the hose and move it about to dislodge air bubbles. Cork or stopper each end when you move the level around.

FINDING THE CONTOUR ON A SLOPE

❊ The base of the 1m rulers or two sticks, which are the same length, have the same vertical height. These positions can be pegged or marked and one ruler, with the hose, can be moved to another position. The hose is moved up or down the slope until the water is once again level with the top of the ruler or stick. Figure 80 illustrates this idea.

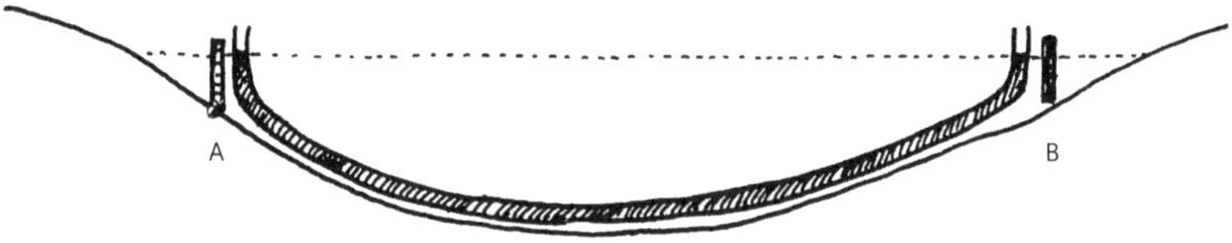

Figure 80. The vertical height at points A and B is the same. These points are said to be on the same contour.

TO DETERMINE THE FALL ON A SLOPE

- Place the 1m rulers 10m apart down the slope.
- Move the other end of the hose up or down until the water level is stationary. Record the height in centimetres (or millimetres).
- Calculate the fall by dividing the difference between the two water levels and the distance between them. For example, in figure 81 the height difference between the water levels is 0.4m and the distance between them is 1m. The fall is then calculated as a ratio of 0.4:10 or 1:25. This means a fall of 1m over 25m of slope.

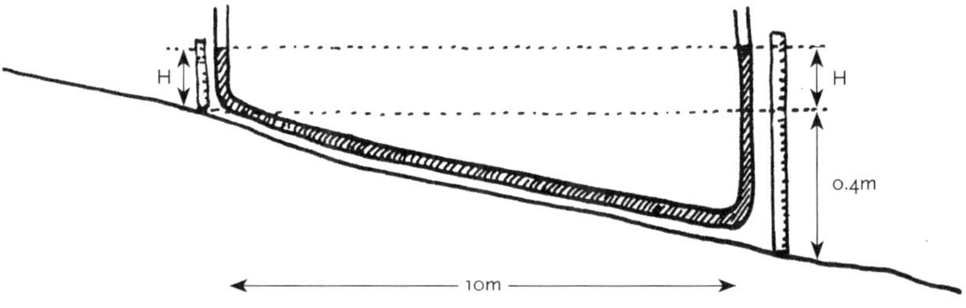

Figure 81. Calculating the fall on a slope. To drain water only needs a fall of 1:400, but 1:200 is most commonly used. Sewage lines often require a fall of 1:60 or more, depending on the local government bylaws.

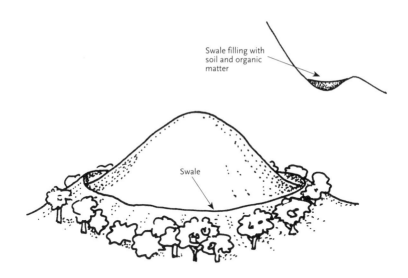

Figure 82. A swale will hold water. Rainfall is captured and can then move into the soil.

From A Permaculture Perspective

Contours are important in permaculture. You need to determine the contour line on a slope to make roads, dams, buildings, drains and even garden beds. You can think of a contour as an imaginary line, where all points along it are at the same height or altitude – it is level.

A contour line is always at right angles (90°) to the slope of the land, so as land changes slope and direction, so too will the contour lines curve and turn.

Garden beds are usually built horizontally. This minimises water drainage, as water will start to flow even on the gentlest of slopes.

To hold water in the landscape, a swale is sometimes constructed. This is essentially a small ditch which holds water and allows it to penetrate into the soil rather than draining it away. Swales are useful strategies for sandy areas as the water can penetrate the soil. Figure 82 illustrates the concept of a swale.

Propagating Plants

Many plants can be easily propagated. You will reduce the cost of the product you are growing if you harvest and germinate your own seeds. Once you have mastered some of the following techniques you will be able to find out about other propagation techniques such as aerial layering and grafting.

Making Labels

You can buy plastic labels which you can write on, or you can make your own labels from aluminium cans. (If you do want white plastic labels, you can cut up a 2l ice cream container or its lid.)

What you need

❀ Aluminium cans – beer or soft (cool) drink cans.

❀ Scissors.

❀ Biro (ball point pen).

What you do

❀ Puncture one end of a beer or soft drink can with the scissors.

❀ Carefully cut around the base of the can to remove it.

❀ Repeat this procedure for the other end. Discard both the base and lid (into the recycling bin).

❀ Unroll the aluminium foil and flatten it.

Figure 83. Cut an alumunium can into strips for cheap plant labels.

✤ Cut the foil into thin strips, about 15mm across. You should be able to make about a dozen strips from one can.

✤ Use the biro to write the name of the plant or seedling on the aluminium strip. Press firmly to make a noticeable imprint. You may not be able to see the colour of the biro mark but you should be able to read the imprint.

Collecting Seed

Collecting seeds is one of the easiest techniques that you can master. Collecting your own seeds is very satisfying, and it saves money at the same time.

What you need

✤ Paperbags.

✤ Marker pen and labels.

✤ String or bag ties.

✤ Shadecloth, 2 x 2m.

✤ Wooden, metal or plastic tray.

✤ Used (recycled) envelopes.

✤ Stapler or sticky tape.

What you do

There are three main ways to collect seed.

1. Locate mature flowers of the vegetable, herb or tree you wish to collect seed from. Place a paper bag over the flower, cone or seed head. Secure this in place with a bag tie or string. Do not use a plastic bag as this traps moisture and will cause the growth of moulds.

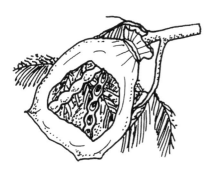

Figure 84. Place a mature flower in a paper bag and collect the seeds as they fall out of the fruit.

As the flower head ripens the seeds are ejected from the fruit and are retained in the paper bag.

2. This method is good for trees which have seed pods which split open. Place a piece of shade cloth (or plastic sheeting) over the ground beneath the tree. Tuck it around the trunk. Gently shake the tree and collect the seeds which fall onto the shadecloth.

3. Pick the mature fruits and flowers of your plants. Place them in a wooden, plastic or metal tray. Usually, you only put one type of plant (flower) in each tray, so that the seeds of different species do not get mixed up. Place the trays in a warm position such as on the back ledge of the car window, in a hothouse or a cold frame (see Hothouses section). Place a label, with the name of the flower or plant, in the tray. As the fruits or pods ripen, they split open and eject the seeds into the tray.

Shade cloth

Figure 85. Shaking a tree will dislodge seeds from their pods.

Place your seeds in an used envelope. Staple or tape the flap down. Write the name of the seeds on the envelope, and list details of location and date. Store the seed packets in a cardboard box or a dark cupboard. The seeds of some species do not last long. Often, they will need to be planted within one year.

Germinating Seed

The seeds of many plants are easy to germinate. A large number of seed sprouts, such as mung beans and alfalfa, are edible and can provide high levels of nutrition. Many other seeds can be germinated for planting in the garden or to increase the range of plants you may be able to sell.

What you need

❋ Seeds.

❋ Marker pen and labels.

❋ Potting mix of soil and compost.

❋ Potting (germinating) trays.

❋ Glass jars.

❋ Hot water.

What you do

❋ Find out if the seed you wish to germinate requires pre-treatment. Some hard seed species, such as acacia, albizzia and tagastaste, should be soaked in hot water for ten minutes or more. Some species need soaking for longer but don't need hot water, and some seeds need chilling for a period of time. Most small, soft vegetable seeds do not need special treatment and can be planted directly into the trays.

❋ Place the potting mixture into a germinating tray. The soil used should be free draining. Add enough to half fill the tray. Tamp down on a bench or use another tray to press the soil into the bottom tray.

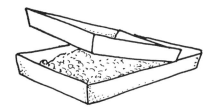

Figure 86. Press the potting mix firmly into the germinating tray.

95

* Sprinkle the seeds over the tray. Very small seeds (e.g. mustard) can be placed in a salt shaker, but most seeds can simply be spread as evenly as possible over the soil. Adding dry sand to the seed envelope and shaking this mixture over the tray is another useful strategy.

* Cover the seeds with more soil. The general rule of thumb is: cover the seeds with soil to a depth that is about the seed size. In other words, small seeds only require a thin layer of soil over them. Large seeds, such as pumpkin, should be buried deeper.

* Place a label of the type of seeds in the tray.

* Water the tray by gently spraying water from a hose, or use a watering can to thoroughly wet the potting mix. Seedlings need to be watered frequently – once or twice a day. Do not let the soil in the tray become dry.

* After seedlings germinate and grow to about 5cm, transplant them into the garden or into larger (deeper) pots.

Figure 87. Water seedlings frequently.

Cuttings

A 'cutting' is a piece of stem or root that can develop into a new plant. It is an example of vegetative reproduction, and is a technique frequently employed in the horticultural industry to produce large numbers or copies of a particular plant stock.

What you need

* Cup or jar.

* Marker pen and labels.

❁ Metal or plastic tray.

❁ Secateurs or scissors.

❁ Hormone powder or gel, or honey (optional: fresh cutting of willow species).

❁ Potting mix.

❁ Tube pots (newspaper or plastic).

❁ Selection of herbs, such as rosemary, lavender, scented pelargoniums.

What you do

❁ Using scissors or secateurs cut the tips off a stock herb plant. You usually only need the top 5-6cm of a branch. Place these directly into a cup of water, until you are ready for the next step.

❁ Take one cutting and strip or cut most of the leaves off. Reduce the size of any large leaves remaining.

❁ Dip the cut end into hormone striking powder or gel. These products are numbered and used according to the type of plant and the degree of soft-wood or hardwood. Check with the supplier for your particular requirements. Number 2 striking medium is a good general purpose medium and is satisfactory for most soft herbs.

❁ Alternatively, dip your cutting into honey or a solution of freshly mashed willow twig in water – the natural plant

Figure 88. Cutting material should be trimmed of most of its leaves and cut to a size about 5cm long.

97

hormones ooze out of the willow (any willow will do) and instigate root development in the cutting. These techniques often work just as well as commercial mediums.

- Place the cutting into a freely draining soil mix in a 50mm tube or flower pot (or even the newspaper pots you made on page 22).

Figure 89. Leave the cutting to develop roots for some time before you transplant it.

- Keep the soil in the pot moist by watering once or twice a day.

- During colder months it is best to keep your cuttings in a warm place, such as under a mini-hothouse or cold-frame (see pages 55 - 56).

- Not all plants strike well. Some woody plants require a stronger hormone powder and some native plants cannot be struck easily. It is a matter for you to experiment and see which plants you have success with.

- You will see the cutting growing as new shoots emerge. This is an indication that roots are probably developing. Leave the cutting for a few weeks or more before you transplant or pot on to a larger pot size.

Ground Layering

You have probably noticed that sometimes your shrubby plants have branches drooping onto the ground. When you try to lift them up you see that the branches are anchored by roots into the soil. We can use this property of plants to grow others, in a technique which is called layering. Layering works well with some types of bamboos and many herbs.

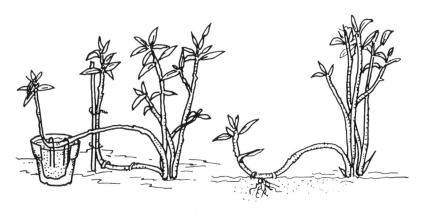

Figure 90. Many plants can be propagated by ground layering.

What you need

❋ Razor blade or knife.

❋ Potting mix or soil.

❋ Stiff fencing wire – for pegs.

❋ Optional: Hormone striking powder or gel.

What you do

❋ Bend one branch and notice where it hits the ground.

❋ Use a knife or razor blade to make a small cut through the bottom part of the outer bark.

❋ Optional: You can dip the cut section into hormone powder or gel, or rub some honey over the cut surface.

❋ Bury the limb, and hold it down with wire pegs. Cover completely with soil.

❋ Keep the plant well watered.

✽ After several weeks, carefully move soil away to inspect the possible development of roots.

✽ After the plant has well developed roots (often after several months) sever the limb from the main plant and transplant or pot up.

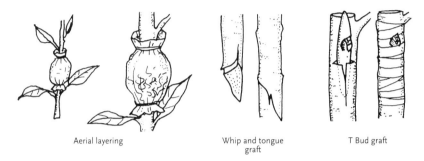

Aerial layering

Whip and tongue graft

T Bud graft

Figure 91. You can find out about aerial layering and grafting which are also used to propagate plants.

From A Permaculture Perspective

Being able to propagate your own plants and knowing how to collect and store seeds are the key skills for any gardener. There are many plants which we can propagate by cuttings or layering, and there will always be plants we have to buy from commercial nurseries (and we should support our local permaculture nurseries and suppliers anyway!

When we collect our own seeds at least we know that they are organically grown and, in many cases, non-hybrid. Non-hybrid seeds are those that are produced by the one species, or one variant, of plant. These seeds are true to form and will normally germinate successfully. These types of plants are the traditional or heirloom varieties that people have always grown.

Some seed manufacturers cross (or hybridise) different plants and varieties to get seeds which grow in the first year and produce fruit, but often the seeds they produce will not themselves grow into new plants – they may be sterile. This effectively means that you have to purchase new seeds every year if you want to grow food.

Collecting and then growing your own seed ensures plants that are best suited to your local climate and soil type.

In some gardens, some flowers and fruits are not picked. These plants are left to self-seed. The seeds fall onto the ground and will germinate when conditions are right. You will find plants popping up everywhere, creating an instant spread of your garden area.

It is very important to record the date that you collected the seed. Seeds you wish to germinate need to be from last season's crop. Many seeds lose their viability after a year or more, and so will not sprout. Remember too that many commercial seed packets contain fungicides and other chemicals to protect the seeds from diseases. Some people are allergic to these substances.

Bird-Attracting Projects You Can Try

Some birds are natural predators of insects. To reduce the incidence of insect attack on our vegetables and plants, we can attract birds to help combat the pests. Besides, birds are just lovely to look at and observe.

Here are some simple projects you can build. The bird feeders are made from either a 2l plastic milk container or a soft drink bottle. These are suitable for small birds. Larger birds may need a flowerpot base like the birdbath shown in figure 93.

The nesting box is best made from timber. Try to position the box in the highest part of a large tree (without falling out and injuring yourself). Don't forget to make a landing or perch outside the entry hole.

If you want one of these pot bases to act as a bird feeder make sure that the birdbath is the lower one – birds love to splash and you shouldn't get the bird seed wet.

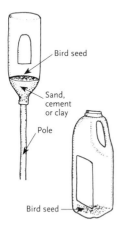

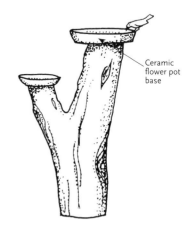

Figure 92. Two types of recycled plastic bottle bird feeders.

Figure 93. Bird bath and / or feeding tray.